FOUNDATIONS OF MODERN ECONOMICS SERIES

Otto Eckstein, *Editor*

MATTHEW EDEL *Queens College, C. U. N. Y.*

Economics
and the Environment

PRENTICE-HALL, INC. *Englewood Cliffs, New Jersey*

Library of Congress Cataloging in Publication Data

EDEL, MATTHEW.
   Economics and the environment.

   (Foundations of modern economics series)
   Bibliography: p.
   1. Environmental policy. 2. Economics.
I. Title.
HC79.E5E32   301.31   72-11799
ISBN 0-13-231316-2
ISBN 0-13-231308-1 (pbk)

For Kim

PRENTICE-HALL FOUNDATIONS
OF MODERN ECONOMICS SERIES

Otto Eckstein, *Editor*

10 9 8 7 6 5 4 3 2 1

PRENTICE-HALL INTERNATIONAL, INC., *London*
PRENTICE-HALL OF AUSTRALIA, PTY., LTD., *Sydney*
PRENTICE-HALL OF CANADA, LTD., *Toronto*
PRENTICE-HALL OF INDIA PVT. LIMITED, *New Delhi*
PRENTICE-HALL OF JAPAN, INC., *Tokyo*

Foundations

of Modern Economics Series

Economics has grown so rapidly in recent years, it has increased so much in scope and depth, and the new dominance of the empirical approach has so transformed its character, that no one book can do it justice today. To fill this need, the Foundations of Modern Economic Series was conceived. The Series, brief books written by leading specialists, reflects the structure, content, and key scientific and policy issues of each field. Used in combination, the Series provides the material for the basic one-year college course. The analytical core of economics is presented in *Prices and Markets* and *National Income Analysis*, which are basic to the various fields of application. *The Price System* is a more sophisticated alternative introduction to microeconomics. Two books in the Series, *Evolution of Modern Economics* and *Economic Development: Past and Present*, can be read without prerequisite and can serve as an introduction to the subject.

For the third editions, the books have been thoroughly revised and updated. Topics that have come into the forefront of attention have been added or expanded. To preserve the virtues of brevity, older material has been weeded out. *Managerial Economics* has been added to the Series to show more fully how economic reasoning can be applied to decisions in the business firm.

Economists have focused increasingly in the last few years on the question of the distribution of income and on the economics of the environment. These topics have been viewed from a fundamental critical point of view that examines what characteristics of the economic system produce the shortcomings in economic performance in these regards. The material on income distribution has been expanded in several of the books. In addition, a new volume has been added, *Economies and the Environment*, which presents the analytical foundations of the problem and raises the systems questions.

The Foundation approach enables the instructor to devise his own course curriculum rather than to follow the format of the traditional textbook. Once analytical principles have been mastered, many sequences of topics can be arranged and specific areas can be explored at length. An instructor not interested in a complete survey course can omit some books and concentrate on a detailed study of a few fields. One-semester courses stressing either macro- or micro-economics can be readily devised. The Instructors Guide to the Series indicates the variety of ways the books in the Series can be used.

This Series is an experiment in teaching. The continued positive response has encouraged us to continue to develop this new approach. The thoughtful reaction and classroom reports from teachers have helped us once more in preparing the third editions. The Series is used both as a substitute for the basic textbook and as supplementary reading in elementary and intermediate courses.

The books do not offer settled conclusions. They introduce the central problems of each field and indicate how economic analysis enables the reader to think more intelligently about them, in order to make him a more thoughtful citizen and to encourage him to pursue the subject further.

Otto Eckstein, *Editor*

Contents

Economies
and the Environment

Economics

and Ecology

This book explores the relations between two systems of interconnected phenomena. One is the *economy*, a social institution by which human beings determine who will do what work, what they will produce, how they will produce it, and who will consume or use different parts of the product. The other is the *ecosystem*, consisting of the relationships between living organisms and their environments, relationships that are subject to physical, chemical, and biological laws. For years, these systems have been studied by separate scientists: economists and natural ecologists. This separation between the two studies has been made obsolete by problems of pollution, resource depletion, and population pressure on food supply. Oil slicks, overfishing, smog, and other growing threats to biological existence have focused attention on the way in which the economy interacts with nature.

Considerations of ecology can be added to those of economics to study some of the relations between economic growth and institutions and the ecological crisis. Problems of food supply and population growth in less-developed areas and issues of pollution and conservation that arise with economic development are studied in this book. The emphasis is on how the economy and environment interact and on how the rules and institutions of the economy can affect these interactions.

This first chapter introduces the way in which economics and ecology developed as separate sciences, studying what were thought of as separate systems of cause and effect. Economists and ecologists learned from each other even before they had to focus on common problems. Their two sciences developed similar approaches. Each describes the systems studied in terms of flows of materials, goods, or wealth. Each seeks to

1

show how balance or equilibrium comes about in these flows. Each shows how growth or evolution over time can alter these balances. In some ways, they differ. Economics has the more direct framework in the study and evaluation of human choice; ecology, the greater sensitivity to issues of survival.

TWO POPULATIONS; TWO SYSTEMS

Snowshoe hares are small animals that live in northern Canada. The Hudson Bay Company kept track of the number of skins brought to trading posts. Their records show that the number of snowshoe hares rose and fell regularly over many decades, with each cycle of the population averaging between nine and ten years in length. Cattle are larger animals that live, among other places, on the grasslands of Argentina. The Argentine government takes censuses of livestock, and keeps records of the number of cattle slaughtered. These records show that the number of cattle rises and falls like the population of Canadian hares. When the fluctuations of the two populations are graphed, as in Figs. 1–1 and 1–2, the two figures appear to be similar. However, the reasons for the fluctuations of the two populations are different.

The number of hares fluctuates for two important reasons. One is the supply of food. When the hare population increases, plants become scarce from their feeding. Starvation sets in, and many hares die. A smaller population survives on the food that remains until plants regrow, and the hare population starts to increase again. A second reason for fluctuation may be the number of

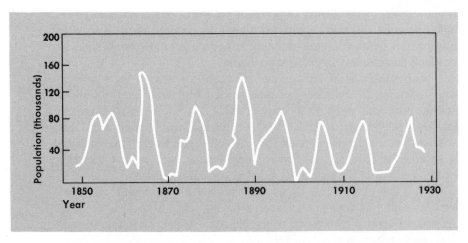

FIG. 1–1 Population of snowshoe hare. (Source: Edward J. Kormondy, *Concepts of Ecology* (Englewood Cliffs, N. J.: Prentice-Hall, Inc., 1959), p. 96. Redrawn from D. A. MacLulich, 1937. University of Toronto Studies, Biological Series No. 43. Based on records of pelts received by the Hudson Bay Company.)

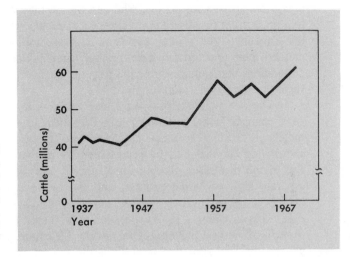

FIG. 1–2 Argentine cattle herd size. (Source: Lovell S. Jarvis, *Supply Response in the Cattle Industry: The Argentine Case.* Ph.D. dissertation, Massachusetts Institute of Technology, 1969, p. 203. Herd size calculated from Argentine government cattle census and slaughter data.)

hares eaten by the lynx. The number of lynx pelts received by the Hudson Bay Company moves in phase with the number of hare skins. As the number of hares increases, these predators' diet improves and their population increases. With more cats to hunt them, the hare population may be kept from further growth.

The Argentine cattle herd does not grow or shrink because of changes in its food supply. Grass is abundant. Argentine ranchers know enough about range management to keep the number of cattle from outrunning the food supply and causing starvation. Nor do herds fluctuate because of changing numbers of predators. Argentine beef is eaten by the people of Buenos Aires and London. The number of Argentines and Englishmen does not fluctuate as the lynx population does. It cannot explain the fluctuating number of cattle.

What does affect the cattle population is the price of beef. When meat is expensive, ranchers find it worthwhile to spend money and effort fattening more steers. The population of cattle rises when ranchers expect prices to be favorable. On the other hand, when prices are low and ranchers expect them to remain low, the effort of raising cattle is less attractive. The ranchers reduce the size of their herds, selling off some of their animals for whatever they will bring, to reduce the costs of running their spreads.

In their causes, fluctuations of the Argentine cattle population resemble fluctuations in Detroit automobile production more than they do fluctuations of hares in Canada. Manufacturers also increase production when they expect to be able to sell large quantities of their product at high prices. When demand falls, they will either produce less because of the low prices, or (if they are monopolists) reduce production to keep prices high. Like automobiles, Argentine cattle increase in numbers because people increase their demand for them. Producers see this increased demand reflected in high prices and decide to in-

3

crease output. Unlike people, who can decide they want more beef and achieve that production by raising more cows (or inducing others, by paying them more), the Canadian lynx cannot decide to increase rabbit production. If lynxes increased their appetite for hares, rather than inducing an increase in the hare population, like Londoners bidding up the beef price, they would cause a more rapid decline in their food supply.

The two populations—hares and cattle—can each be analyzed. In either case, changes in the population can be shown to occur systematically and not merely as random accidents. In each case, the causes of the changes can be shown; indeed, they can be represented by mathematical or computer models. But in the two cases, the causes of change are different. Each results from a separate kind of causal process; and the two causal processes involved have been investigated by two separate sciences. The system of causal relationships that explains changes in the population of hares is the subject of *ecology*, a branch of natural science. The system of causal relationships that explains changes in the population of cattle is the subject of *economics*, a branch of social science.

The Development of Two Sciences

Sciences develop around questions. Sometimes, these questions point to long research agendas. Often, a scientific breakthrough consists essentially of asking a new and important question, which leads to a new perception of how the world works. Economics developed around questions concerning the causes of change in prices and trading patterns, the efficient use of resources, the wealth of different nations, the distribution of wealth, and the policies that affect these. Ecology developed around questions about the interrelationships between different species of plants and animals and the ways in which living populations interacted with their environments. Today, scientists face new concerns over human population, hunger, congestion, pollution, and conservation. Such concerns suggest new questions about the way in which human beings and their economies interact with the natural environment. These questions suggest bringing together the disciplines that have investigated the relevant causal systems as separate units. Economics and ecology will have to work together to find answers.

This will not be the first time economics and ecology have learned from each other. They already share common features as studies of patterns of cause and effect in interconnected systems. Their names both derive from the same Greek word for "household management." Even if they have turned their attentions respectively to nature's management of the "earth household" and to man's management of society's provisioning, ecology and economics have built on each other's ways of looking at reality. They also shared some common questions in the early stages of their development.

In 1786, a British pamphleteer named Joseph Townshend was attacking the "Poor Laws," which granted relief to poor families. Like some present day critics of welfare programs, Townshend feared the laws would encourage the

4

poor to have too many children. However, he did not make that claim straight off. Rather, he told how a Spanish ship left some goats on an island. At first, the goats lived an idyllic existence, for there was plentiful food on the island. But eventually, their population grew so that they could no longer find enough to eat.

> In this situation, the weakest gave way first and plenty was again restored. Thus they fluctuated between happiness and misery, and either suffered want or rejoiced in abundance, according to whether their numbers were diminished or increased; never at a stay yet nearly balancing at all times their quantity of food.[1]

Later, English privateers began hunting the goats for food while preparing to attack Spanish ships. So the Spanish introduced dogs to eat the goats. At first, the dogs multiplied because of the abundant meat. The number of goats diminished, but the population was not destroyed completely; some goats escaped onto the rocky hills. Dogs could only catch the goats when they came down for food. Only the "careless and the rash" goats were caught; only the most "watchful, strong and active" dogs could get enough food. Thus, a new balance was established that not only allowed the survival of some dogs and goats but also ensured that the survivors would be the best of their species.

Townshend argued by analogy that assistance to the poor would encourage the breeding of the least hard working and burden the more industrious with taxes. He said the "Poor Law" led both to an expansion of the population and a lowering of the quality of Englishmen. This argument assumed that the poor were unemployed because of their own personal indolence and not because of the way in which British society was organized. This assumption is questionable, and Townshend never justified it. Nonetheless, his description of a balanced natural system, in which the population of goats and dogs regulated and improved each other, was influential.

Ten years earlier, Adam Smith showed, in *The Wealth of Nations*, that competition between different producers could regulate the price at which they could sell and lead to economic growth by enforcing efficiency on the businesses. This, too, was a view of a society as a system that was both regulated and improved by the interaction between different elements in it. The ideas of both Smith and Townshend were used by Thomas Robert Malthus to construct a new description of a system in which human population, nature, and the economy interacted. Where Smith and Townshend saw competition as allowing improvement of the economy or of goat and dog populations, Reverend Malthus mistrusted any faith in progress. He argued economic improvement would lead to population growth, so that mankind would always be faced with starvation, unless some other form of destruction limited population.

The notion of competition for resources was used by Charles Darwin to

5

---

[1] Joseph Townshend, "A Dissertation on the Poor Laws" (1786), in *Population, Evolution and Birth Control*, Garrett Hardin, ed. (San Francisco: W. W. Freeman, 1969), pp. 24–27.

explain the evolution of species in nature. Darwin knew the ways in which gardeners and horse breeders exercised selection to encourage the breeding of plants and animals with desirable traits. Then, he later wrote,

> I happened to read for amusement Malthus on population. And being well prepared to appreciate the struggle for existence which everywhere goes on, from long-continued observation of the habits of animals and plants, it at once struck me that under these circumstances favorable variations would tend to be preserved, and unfavorable ones to be destroyed.[2]

This competitive mechanism of "natural selection" became the basis for Darwin's theory of evolution.

Darwin's work, in turn, was used by economists to argue that competition, by ensuring the "survival of the fittest," would ensure economic progress. These "social Darwinists" used their arguments to oppose assistance to the poor. Their optimism about the evolution of the economic system, given a regimen of competition, gave economics a complacent outlook about society. The general tenor of the science, for many years, became one of an examination of the balance that competition brought about, and a justification of any equilibrium that resulted as being necessarily the best for society. Concern for the consequences of the economic progress for both poverty and nature was neglected by most economists.

One exception was the work of Karl Marx. He tried to refute Malthus, arguing that poverty resulted from capitalistic institutions and exploitation, not from population growth. In opposition to idealist views of humanity, he stressed that human society was based in the natural world and that the economy was affected by, and itself affected, nature. Most important, he used the idea of evolution to develop a theory of history, in which the economy and society passed from feudalism to capitalism and from capitalism to socialism in response to the development of production. Marx even offered to dedicate *Capital* to Darwin. However, except for Thorstein Veblen and other "institutionalists," few economists followed the lead of examining the evolution of the economy, and Marxists themselves lost interest, for many years, in the impact of the economy on nature.

Notions of equilibrium or balance, meanwhile, were borrowed back from economics by students of natural history. The term *ecology* was proposed by Ernst Haeckel, who explained

> . . . by ecology we mean the body of knowledge concerning the economy of nature—the investigation of the total relations of the animal both to its inorganic and to its organic environment, including above all, its friendly and inimical relation with those animals and plants with which it comes directly or indirectly into contact—in a word, ecology is the study of all the complex interrelations referred to by Darwin as the 'conditions of the struggle for existence'.[3]

[2] Charles Darwin, *Autobiography* (1876), *ibid.*, p. 147.

[3] Ernst Haeckel (1870) in Edward J. Kormondy, *Concepts of Ecology* (Englewood Cliffs, N. J.: Prentice-Hall, 1969), p. viii.

The effects of human activity on the environments facing plant and animal species were part of these conditions, and some naturalists investigated them. The development of ecology as a research science revolved around studies of the functioning of fairly isolated and small natural ecological systems: the interrelationships among species in bogs, tundras, or other habitats

The detachment of ecology and economics has ended in recent years, under the impact of modern industry, agriculture, transport, and warfare. Ecologists find that more and more of the ecosystems they study are affected by economic activities. Economists discover that natural limits of food supply, materials availability, or waste dispersal are disrupting the systems they study. Economics and ecology developed as separate but similar sciences; now they must borrow each other's specific findings to answer their own questions.

Discovering Interconnections

Some of the first investigations of the effects of human activity on the environment were carried out in the nineteenth century. George Perkins Marsh, a diplomat, classical scholar, and Fisheries Commissioner of Vermont, showed how the development of Western Europe and the United States had led to the destruction of forests. Land was cleared for farming and wood cut for construction and fuel (or wasted). The removal of forests had altered climates; led to drought, or to erosion, in some areas; and left some lands unusable for crops or habitation in the long run. He deduced these influences from his own experiences in New England as forests were removed and from a comparison of ancient descriptions of European regions with their current conditions.

Marsh also showed how the economy was affecting the character of the woods, even where man did not fell the trees directly. Bogs within the forest, he argued, were often formed when beavers obstructed small streams with their dams. These created ponds that allowed the growth of aquatic plants. Eventually, the ponds filled with vegetable wastes, becoming swampy places in which still other plants and animals could live. The growth of the fur trade led to the drying up of bogs because of the destruction of beavers.

So long as the fur of the beaver was extensively employed as a material for fine hats, it bore a very high price, and . . . naturalists feared its speedy extinction. When a Parisian manufacturer invented the silk hat, which soon came into almost universal use, the demand for beavers' fur fell off, and this animal—whose habits as we have seen, are an important agency in the formation of bogs and other modifications of forest nature—immediately began to increase. . . . Thus the convenience or the caprice of Parisian fashion has unconsciously exercised an influence which may sensibly affect the physical geography of a distant continent.[4]

[4] George Perkins Marsh, *Man and Nature* (1864). (Cambridge, Mass.: Harvard University Press, 1965), p. 76.

7

The distant or local environmental effects of the trade in hats or the expansion of farming are often not taken into account by the people who decide on these economic activities. However, the destruction of forests, the clogging of lakes as a result of use of detergents, or the destruction of animal species as a result of temporary fashions may do long-run damage to natural environments and species and also interrupt later economic activities.

In recent years, more interrelations have become apparent. Urbanization, industrialization, and growing levels of waste leave few areas free of human influence. A larger proportion of economic output now consists of products not found spontaneously in nature. Barry Commoner has argued this "technological displacement" means that a larger number of products can do damage to ecosystems.[5] Supplying a growing population with food and growing industries with materials and energy have become problems, as has preventing damage done by waste products. Ecologists find their studies must consider the effects of these products and activities. Economists realize they must take ecological effects into account when they estimate the costs or benefits of different activities. Both sciences realize they must also discover the lines of causality that run between human society and nature, and involve the working of both human institutions and natural laws, if they are to understand the problems we face.

The Need for Models

How are the relations to be studied? The changes that a science seeks to explain may be observable in many ways. Many of the causal interrelationships within a system may not be observable directly. The investigator must infer them from visible data, combining a plausible theory—a model or paradigm—with the observations to describe how relationships occur. Not all correlations in nature are evidence for direct causality. Common sense and careful specification of each step in a suggested causal explanation, often by means of a mathematical version of the model, can, however, establish presumptions of the patterns of causality. Statisticians observe that sales of ice cream and boating accidents move in cycles that are parallel. Does this mean that eating ice cream causes careless boating, as drinking causes careless driving? More likely, both the eating of ice cream and the total number of people using boats go up during heat waves. Separate lines of causation, from temperature to ice cream consumption, and from temperature to boating to accidents, can be presumed to exist.

Statisticians also find cigarette smoking in individuals to be correlated with cancer and heart disease. Does this mean smoking causes disease, or does it mean that another physical, emotional, or occupational factor increases both the need of an individual to smoke and the probability of illness? Neither pattern can be ruled out on the grounds of common sense. More complicated statistical

[5] Barry Commoner, *The Closing Circle: Nature, Man and Technology* (New York: Alfred A. Knopf, 1971), Chap. 9.

tests of the relation between various presumed third factors and smoking and disease were needed before most statisticians were convinced that smoking did increase the risk of disease. Even then, not all statisticians find the evidence strong enough to convince them.

To interpret reality, hypotheses are needed. Plausible models of systems of cause and effect must be imagined and then tested against observation. Both economics and ecology have developed such models. Townshend's notion of balance between dogs and goats, Adam Smith's vision of competition leading to progress, and the other examples discussed in the previous section are hypotheses about causation. Economics and ecology, as sciences, consist of sets of such hypotheses.

The two sciences have some similarities. Both economists and ecologists study the pieces of reality that concern them as *systems*; configurations whose different parts interrelate and affect each other and within which causes and effects, structures, and functions can be traced. Both use notions that are similar in three respects: the tracing of *flows* of inputs and outputs through systems; the analysis of how *equilibrium* or balance is obtained within systems; and the study of the *growth* or development of systems. But, we shall also find, there is one way in which the systems studied by the two sciences are different. Economists study systems in which actions are carried on for what people view as deliberate purposes. Such systems operate according to rules that are amenable to human intervention. Ecologists have focused on whether species or ecosystems will survive or change and sometimes considered them to evolve *as if* choices are being made. Economists lately have begun to learn from ecologists that they have often paid too little attention to viability or evolution. The deliberate choice of systems, and the possibility of planning, are elements that the economist may consider in ways the ecologist cannot.

FLOWS THROUGH A SYSTEM

One similarity between economics and ecology is that both analyze flows between parts of a system. Ecologists study the flow of energy and nutrients between the surrounding environment and different plant and animal populations. Economists study the flow of goods and services between groups of buyers and sellers and between different industries. Either set of flows can be described as a system of input-output relationships, with the *inputs* flowing into the system as a whole (or into population or industry subsystems) bearing a relation to the *outputs* flowing from the system (or its subsystems).

Energy Flow and Food Chains

Ecologists observing a pond, a watershed, an ocean, or a field may begin by measuring the flow of energy through that natural habitat. Some solar energy

9

reaches the surface of the earth's atmosphere and a part of this energy is used by green plants, along with water and carbon dioxide, to produce carbohydrates. These plants then are available as a source of energy to the *primary consumers* of the ecosystem, the herbivorous animals. Some of these, in turn, are eaten by, and provide energy to, carnivores or *secondary consumers*. Some of these may be consumed by still other animals. Plant and animal matter not otherwise eaten is eventually consumed by "decomposers," such as bacteria and fungus.

At each stage, or *trophic level*, of such a food chain, some energy will be wasted, some used for the daily activities of the organism, and some accumulated as increased body weight. This accumulated energy is what is available for the consumption of consumers at higher trophic levels. Thus, in any ecosystem there is less energy available to herbivores than to the green plants or *autotrophs;* less energy available to carnivores than to herbivores. Despite farmers' best efforts at selective breeding, several times as much energy (measured in calories) must be fed to a pig or chicken as the animal will provide in food for human consumers.

Biogeochemical cycles—flows of hydrogen, oxygen, carbon and various nutrient elements between the surrounding environment and populations at different trophic levels—are linked closely to the energy cycle. In photosynthesis, carbon dioxide and water are combined, forming free oxygen that is released into the air and carbohydrates (compounds of hydrogen, carbon, and oxygen) that pass through the food chain. When plants and animals burn these compounds for energy, oxygen from the air is recombined with the organic matter, producing carbon dioxide and water. Water also is retained in the bodies of plants and animals and carbon, hydrogen, and oxygen also form part of more complex organic compounds when combined with other nutrients. The cyclical flows of other nutrient inputs and outputs also can be traced. One important cycle includes the fixation of nitrogen from the atmosphere by certain microorganisms; the utilization of nitrates produced by this fixation (or from organic wastes or fertilizers) by animals and plants at different trophic levels; and the return of nitrogen compounds to the soil or free nitrogen to the atmosphere, through decay. Others involve the passage of sulfur, phosphorus, potassium, calcium, and other elements that must be present for life to exist.

In each cycle, the element is absorbed from some part of the physical environment by a living creature and then acquired by other consumers. Eventually, the element is released into the surrounding environment in processes of decomposition. Any organism requires a large number of nutrients for survival. Therefore, the growth or survival of the population of any species may require the existence of a variety of other species in sufficient numbers from which it can absorb specific elements. In any cycle, the amount of the element returned to the environment in a form suitable for reuse may be as great as the amount absorbed. However, some of the elements may be dissipated in unreusable forms. The accumulation of caloric energy and nutrients in the bodies of plants and animals as populations grow and the loss of nutrients from usable forms in different ecosystems represent ways in which the flow, or input-output structure of an ecosystem, is "open." They show that a system may be subject to a net gain or loss in size between different rounds of a cycle.

Interindustry Flows and Input-Output

Economists, too, chart flows between different units of the system they study. Flows occur between different industries. Iron ore passes from the mining industry to steel mills; their products may be used by the auto industry. Its vehicles, in turn, may be utilized by trucking companies, and old trucks may be sold to scrap metal plants. Steel produced from scrap may, in turn, be used to make typewriters. Meanwhile, rubber will be passing from plantations or synthetics factories to tire manufacturers and from them to the truckers. They, in turn, may sell used tires to junk dealers, who sell them to fruit growers who burn them to ward off frost.

Other cycles show exchanges between people and industries, with foods and other consumer goods flowing to families, which, in turn, provide labor to the industries that produce these and other goods. This cycle overlaps with the energy and other nutrient cycles of the ecologists: people take in energy in their food; they expend it both in respiration and in work that requires more energy than a completely inert existence. People also take in other nutrients in their food, and expel them as body wastes. These, along with unutilized consumer goods and other scraps of products, are returned to the natural environment, as solid wastes, sewage, or smoke.

Economists, like ecologists, consider the input requirements for different industries. Just as each consumer species may require many nutrient sources, so an automobile factory requires steel, chrome, and rubber, as well as labor and electricity. These, in turn, require other inputs in their production. The economist traces the flow between industries and estimates the requirements of each industry for the existence of other industries by means of an *Input-Output Table*.

Table 1–1 is an input-output matrix. The activities of each industry are represented by both a row and a column. Each row shows the uses to which the production of an industry is put. For example, in Table 1–1 the row for the agricultural industry includes entries for the quantity of agricultural and forest products going to the machinery industry (as inputs, like wood for crates); to the consumer goods industries (as inputs, like cotton for textiles); back to agriculture (as inputs, like seeds); to households (directly, as food); into accumulation of inventories; and as exports. The sum of entries in the row is total food production. The columns "exports," "new inventories," and "households" make up "final demand" or outputs not directly used as inputs by other industries.

Each column shows the sources of inputs used in an industry. For the agricultural industry, the column includes the inputs from agriculture already mentioned (seeds, and so on); inputs from the machinery industry (tractors);

11

Table 1-1 INPUT-OUTPUT FLOWS IN AN ECONOMY

Industry or Other Source of Inputs	Consumer of Output						Total Output of Producer
	Agriculture	Machinery Industry	Consumer Good Industry	Exports	New Inventories	Households	
Agriculture	50	200	300	50	100	300	1000
Machinery industry	150	200	100	150	0	0	600
Consumer good industry	50	0	0	50	100	500	700
Imports	150	0	100				250
Labor	400	100	100				600
Profit	200	100	100				400
Total input by consumer or final destination	1,000	600	700	250	200	800	200

All units measured in dollars at the prices prevailing when table is compiled.

12

from households (labor); and from imports, if any. In Table 1–1, there are no inputs into agriculture from consumer goods industries, although there are inputs or flows from agriculture to the consumer goods industries. The sum of the entries in a column poses some problems. Although in any row all the entries could be considered units of the same product, each entry in a column represents a product from a different industry. To add up a column, these different goods must be compared using a common measurement: money values. The sum of a column (the value of the inputs into each industry) is not necessarily the same as the sum of that industry's row (the value of its production), unless profits are included in the table as a separate row. Any money left over from the sale of products that has not gone for the purchase of inputs remains as profits for an industry; thus, the sum of profits plus input prices must balance the value of output.

Using the table, it is possible to calculate the average value of each input used directly in the production of a dollar's worth of each output. This is done by dividing a number in the matrix into the sum at the bottom of the column in which it appears. For example, in Table 1–1, dividing each entry in the agriculture column into the sum at the bottom shows that each dollar's worth of agricultural products requires fifteen cents worth of machinery inputs, fifteen cents of imports, forty cents of labor, five cents of other agricultural products, and five cents of consumer products as inputs.

The amount of each product required *directly and indirectly* for a dollar's worth of every other product can also be computed. Thus, the machinery used in our dollar's worth of agricultural production itself requires two and one-half cents worth of labor, five cents of agricultural products, and five cents of machinery. These, in turn, use still more inputs of labor and other products.

Tracing all these chains of required inputs is a long process. It can, however, be done quickly by a computer, once the original input-output table is given, using a mathematical technique called "inverting a matrix." This computes the average amount of every product used, directly or indirectly, in the making of a dollar's worth of every other product. The economist can use these averages to predict how much all industries would have to expand to increase production in any one industry by a dollar's worth, or to increase sales to final demand (households, exports, and new inventories) by a dollar. The prediction will be correct as long as the direct input requirement averages of each industry do not change.

The input-output table thus provides a useful summary of flows of goods in an economy, as well as a way of calculating the necessary relations between outputs of different sectors. Its uses will be shown in Chapter 4, where the fuel requirements of a number of industries are discussed.[6]

---

[6] The ecologist's description of energy flows in a system can also be stated in the form of an input-output table. The amounts stated would be in calories, rather than dollars, but the same technique of tracing flows and "inverting the matrix" could be used to calculate the numbers of green plants and herbivores required to support a number of carnivores.

EQUILIBRIUM IN A SYSTEM

Input-output and flow relationships show how different populations or industries supply each others' needs. If the average relations shown in an input-output table represent necessary requirements for production, the table can be used to show a kind of balance that must exist between different industries or populations if the system is to be maintained. There must be herbivores for tigers to eat; there must be machine shops and farms to supply the looms and cotton to the textile mills. But a description of flows does not indicate how this balance is brought about. Does production of deer increase in order to supply the tigers, or production of cotton increase in order to supply the textile mills? Or, do the mills close down or the tigers starve for want of inputs? Both economists and ecologists use a notion of equilibrium to refer to a situation in which different populations or industries are in balance with each other and with resources; both have analyzed mechanisms by which equilibriums may come about.

Market Supply and Demand

One means to establish equilibrium between different industries or between production and consumption is the *market mechanism* or the price system.[7] Prices serve to signal industries whether to expand or contract their production; they may induce consumers to increase or decrease their consumption. The economist's analysis of supply and demand in a competitive market shows how such changes can achieve equilibrium. In Fig. 1–3, the demand curve D represents the relationship between different prices and the quantities of a product that consumers are willing to buy at those prices. At higher prices, they will buy less. A supply curve S shows the quantities that producers offer for sale at different prices. Higher prices usually allow profitable production of larger quantities. At some price P_e, the two curves intersect, and the quantity supplied and the quantity demanded are equal (Q_e). At higher prices, more is to be supplied than purchased; producers compete with each other for sales by lowering prices. This, in turn, increases the quantity demanded and leads to a reduction in production. Eventually, the price is forced down to that level at which the curves intersect. Similarly, the competition of different would-be purchases drives prices up if the quantity demanded exceeds the quantity supplied. At the intersection of the curves, supply and demand are in equilibrium: neither producers nor consumers have an incentive to change the quantity bought or sold.

Economists frequently make use of a presumed property of nature to ex-

[7] Planning is an alternative mechanism. The two have different strengths and weaknesses for the organization of an economy, which are discussed in Chapter 7.

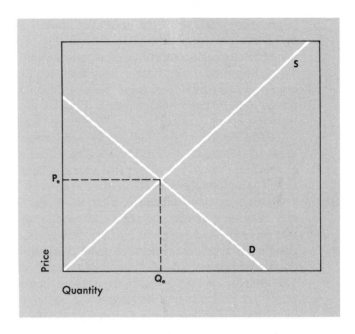

FIG. 1–3 Interaction of supply and demand.

plain why markets achieve equilibrium. This is the principle of *diminishing returns*. Society's ability to use resources has limits, at least in the absence of technological improvement. The supply of diamonds of more than a certain size is limited absolutely by the number of gems in existence. The production of other goods becomes more costly as the quantity produced increases because resources used must be stretched thinner. Increasing the quantity of food produced may require putting more land of lower quality into production. More effort is required to produce on this poorer land, so the cost of a ton of food rises. Alternatively, more labor can be used on existing farms, so that production is increased by more frequent cultivation. But normally, the amount each additional laborer adds to production will be less. In either case, the cost of a product rises as the quantity increases. This is one reason for the usual upward slope of the supply curve. (Similarly, the downward sloping shape of a demand curve may be due to a psychological diminishing return. As a consumer eats more of the same food, he may become bored with it and only demand more if it becomes cheaper. However, demand curves may slope downward because at lower prices more people can afford to consume a product, whatever their psychology.)

An economy with upward sloping supply curves and downward sloping demand curves is more likely to be stable than an economy without them. If, at high prices, the demand curve were to the right of the supply curve (and, at low prices, the supply curve were to the right), there would still be an equilibrium price at which the quantity supplied equaled the quantity demanded. This price would be the price at which the two curves crossed. At higher prices, however, competition would drive the price ever upward because demand exceeded supply. Below the equilibrium price, the quantity supplied would exceed the quantity demanded, and competition of suppliers would drive prices downward. Prices would always be driven further away from equilibrium, unless the economy was exactly at this equilibrium point. Natural diminishing returns, by making a supply curve of that sort unlikely, allow a market to move back toward equilibrium when it is out of balance.

The market analysis of supply and demand shows how one flow in an economy is brought into equilibrium. The output of one sector becomes the input of another, consuming, sector; the price mechanism lets the amounts be equalized. The equilibration of all the flows in an input-output table to form a *general equilibrium* is more difficult to analyze. If markets are not competitive, there may be several possible equilibria, depending on the strategic maneuvers that take place between buyers and sellers. Nor do all markets necessarily achieve an equilibrium relationship between their component sectors. Oscillations of production and prices around an equilibrium may occur. For example, if the available quantity of corn exceeds the amount demanded, its price will fall. Low prices will reduce supply, or increase the quantity demanded, so equilibrium can be achieved. The low prices may reduce supply too much, however. If farmers are discouraged from planting the crop the next year by the low prices, the following harvest season may see a shortage of corn, which leads to very high prices. These, in turn, may induce overplanting and a glut of corn (and low prices) the next year. Cycles in the demand for manufactured goods such as automobiles and general business cycles in the economy are also possible. In one sense, at each point in these cycles markets are equilibrated because prices keep adjusting as required to allow disposal of goods already produced or to ration them among buyers. But these short-run equilibria do not lead to stable prices or quantities produced in the different industries. A longer-run equilibrium is usually defined as existing only when sectors are in balance, so that markets are left without oversupply or excess demand in such a way that prices and quantities can be stable.

Equilibrium in Ecosystems

Populations of different species in natural environments are limited by equilibrating processes that are, in some ways, similar to markets. If populations are too large for resources, competition for food will result in some or all of their members not receiving sufficient nutrients. The population will tend to decline. If there is sufficient nutrition, the numbers will be able to expand. This may lead, as in Townshend's example of the goats, to a balance between population and resources. The diminishing of food availability may lead only some individuals to perish, so that population stabilizes, and perhaps even the most healthy individuals survive. But this is not always a reliable method of regulation for the achievement of a stable population. In some cases, food shortage may weaken or kill so many individuals simultaneously that the entire population declines very rapidly, far below the equilibrium point.

Other natural mechanisms may increase the stability of populations. As examination of food chains indicates, a species normally will be food for some predator, as well as a consumer of nutrients. Predation is sometimes more effective than famine for the selective removal of weak individuals from a population without destruction of the entire group. Selective shortage of nutrients may limit the reproduction of some species when their numbers begin to press on resources but before population reaches limits that would lead to general famine. Population density beyond certain limits may also interrupt the normal "social" patterns of interaction between members of the same species, so that breeding is limited. Or, beyond certain densities of population, the chemical wastes emitted by some species may become concentrated enough that they inhibit growth. Combinations of these mechanisms with the simple limitation of energy have been shown to lead to stable equilibria in the size of many plant and animal populations.

GROWTH AND STRUCTURAL CHANGE IN SYSTEMS

The equilibrium in a market is based on the existence of supply and demand relationships. The supply of a product at different prices depends on the availability of resources, on technology, and on other relationships in the economy. Demand at each price may depend on consumer tastes and on income and its distribution. Similarly, balance between a population, its food supply, and its predators may depend on a number of background factors. The food supply may depend on the availability of nutrients in the soil or upon the weather. The effectiveness of the species in evading its predators may depend on topography or the availability of plants that give it cover. In either a natural ecosystem or in an economy, a balance or equilibrium can only be considered in light of these background conditions.

The background conditions for equilibrium may themselves change, however. Such a change may be imposed from outside the nation or a local natural environment that an economist or an ecologist is studying, and appear to upset a stable equilibrium. Sometimes, however, the internal workings of the system itself may include some slowly developing changes that do not appear important, for a long time, to patterns of prices and outputs in different industries or to the size and relations of different populations. These internally generated changes may eventually reach a level at which they alter the background conditions for equilibrium. New technologies may be developing slowly in the laboratories of a stable industry; nutrients may be slowly washing away from a mountainside in which different plant and animal populations have been in equilibrium. In either case, the equilibrium apparent to the observer may exist within a longer-run disequilibrium. Economists and ecologists both have studied how these long-

17

run changes occur and lead one equilibrium to give way to another, one pattern of relations to be replaced by a successor.

Ecologists call the replacement of one short-run equilibrium by another *"succession.* A simple example is the changing population on land-fills or on plowed or burned-over land. In this empty environment, small plants soon take hold, their seeds brought by wind and water or carried by birds. These first inhabitants are what ecologists call *generalized* species—those highly tolerant of a variety of environments. They provide food and cover for other species, and alter the composition and texture of the soil. This allows new specialized species to survive. If not interrupted by human action or by changes in climate, the succession of species results in an equilibrium more stable than those that preceded it, a *steady state.* Ecologists call such a system, which will not change further through internally induced succession, a *climax community.*

Not all succession results in similar climax communities. Climate, topography, geological composition of the soil, and other factors determine where deciduous forests, coniferous forests, grasslands, tundra, and other ecological communities can emerge. Thus, changes in climate and other disruptions can lead to the replacement of even a stable or climax community by other ecological communities. But some generalizations can be made about climax communities as opposed to the temporary, less-developed states of short-run equilibrium that may precede them.

The greater number of species in climax ecosystems is the first of these generalizations. A second is that environments become more stable the more species they contain and the more complex their relations of competition or predation are. In an empty field with few species, a change in salinity or a high wind may destroy all the plants. A disease that destroys one species may destroy the entire biotic community. In a fully developed climax community, although the individual species are more specialized than those in simpler ecosystems, each species may not exercise the full range of activities of which it is capable. Because of the competition of other species, one carnivore may not eat every species that it could consume. A plant that might be food for several species of herbivore may be utilized little by some of them that find other food more easily. If one species is removed by disease, other species may replace its functions, allowing others to survive. Sometimes, one species may replace another (as the long-horned cattle replaced the buffalo on the American plains) without destroying the rest of the system.

Although climax communities are more stable than simpler ecosystems, they are not indestructible. If enough species in such an ecosystem are destroyed by climatic changes, fire, or human action, the system will be less easily reestablished than a simpler ecological community. The vulnerability of climax commu-

18

nities to shocks beyond some critical level is another generalization familiar to ecologists and one that has considerable importance for mankind's activities.

A climax ecosystem has stability against minor changes that makes it more probable that each individual plant or animal will live to maturity. Thus, generally there will be a higher ratio of individuals of reproducing age to infants within most species than in successional communities. Lower birth and death rates reduce levels of energy and nutrient use by baby animals and plants that will not survive long. The result of this efficiency is a greater ratio between the weight of all living creatures in the ecosystem (its *biomass*) and the amount of energy entering the system.

The development of an ecological community from its origins to its climax can therefore be reflected by the growth of its biomass, the increasing number of species, and the declining birth and death rates of individual species. Only in the steady state do these statistical indicators become relatively constant; but at each point before that, populations of different species may have been in equilibrium. The numbers of each species will have depended on the supplies of food from lower trophic levels and on the numbers of members of competing species. But these equilibria will have been ones in which new species could enter to cause further change. In the steady state, the ecological community will not have its equilibrium as easily disrupted. Even then, climatic changes, a loss of nutrients washed away by streams, human action, or even the evolution of the local species themselves can threaten it. Any equilibrium must always be seen as resting within a wider disequilibrium.

Economic Growth and Development

An economy may also grow or evolve from one equilibrium to another. The equilibrium between supply and demand in one industry or market may be altered if productive capacity in the industry is increased by new investment or training of new workers. Balance between the different sectors of the economy related by input-output flows may be disrupted by changes in the levels of demand or productivity of one or another sector. Even if effective markets keep the different sectors of the economy in balance with each other, at any moment the economy as a whole may change as the supplies of primary inputs, or "factors of production," or the technologies by which they are utilized evolve.

Economists study a number of causes for this kind of development. Technological innovation, resource discovery and depletion, and population growth all may cause the economy to grow and change. The most attention has been given to changes brought about by investment. In an agricultural economy, the amount of seed or compost put aside for the next year's harvest or the amount of labor devoted to clearing and improving and making new tools affects the ability to produce in subsequent years. Only if the new supplies of capital put aside for future years exactly balance the supplies from previous years used up

19

during a crop cycle can the economy be the same in the future as it was in the past. In a more complex economy, the level of production in the industries that produce machinery and the amount put into inventories will affect the future ability of the economy to produce. The more total investment there is, the greater the ability of the economy to produce and consume in the future.

Economists have described a variety of patterns by which economies might grow because of accumulation. They have shown that under some circumstances accumulation will be limited by diminishing returns to capital, so that growth must come to an end once some level of income is achieved. In other cases, technological change might allow permanent growth at a steady rate. Because the ability of nature to supply food, minerals, and other inputs, or to absorb wastes, may be a cause of diminishing returns, economists are now looking to ecologists for advice on which of these hypotheses is adequate.

Economic growth also changes the balance between different sectors of the economy and alters the equilibria of different markets. Generally, as an economy grows and as production per capita increases, changes occur in its input-output structure. The number of industries and products increases; there is more scope for production of luxury goods as well as the bare necessities of life; the proportion of the national effort devoted to agriculture declines. In the process, prices of different products may change, even though at any point markets may be in equilibrium. Growth also affects the relations between the economy and its ecological environment. Population growth rates may rise or fall. Growth increases the ability of the economy to produce foods and hence reduce the chance of famine. But at the same time, it may lead to greater consumption of fuel and the concentration of population into cities, increasing the danger of pollution.

Economic growth may also bring about changes in the institutions of society. The first development of technology to the point at which societies could produce more than was necessary just to subsist and to replace used-up tools had to occur before complicated societies could develop, complete with specialized artisans and a leisure class who lived off the labor of others. More advanced technologies and the accumulation of equipment by society led to further evolution of social institutions in the course of history. Even within economies that seem to be in equilibrium, there may be forces for change. In a capitalist economy, for example, the competition between companies leads to a continual search for new technologies; competition and the presence of profits give businessmen an incentive to search for new investment opportunities. Their investments lead to pressures for new laws, to the consolidation of separate companies into conglomerates, to the rise and decline of communities when different economic activities are possible, and to changes in the conditions under which work takes place. Growth can change supply and demand conditions directly; it may also lead to new attitudes, aspirations, or balances of interests that may cause changes in the basic institutions of the economy. Although most economists perform their analyses on the assumption that the economic rules of the game are "given," there have always been economists who pointed out that economic equilibrium, too, takes place within a framework of change.

VIABILITY AND CHOICE

Economics and ecology both view their domains of study as systems of cause and effect. Both consider flows between interconnected subsystems, equilibrium, and growth in similar ways. In some respects, nonetheless, economics differs from ecology. Economics is concerned with the purposeful action of humans, and human beings can pursue a variety of goals. They may decide on different patterns of consumption or of work and leisure within some set of institutions; they may alter the institutions by which their activities are organized. Economists must consider the possibility of changes in the goals and decisions of individuals that occur more rapidly than the changes in behavior of an animal or plant species that biological evolution brings about. They may inquire as to how well institutions serve the goals of people, whether individuals' actions frustrate or serve their goals, and whether resource use is efficient in terms of its contribution to fulfilling social goals. On the other hand, economics has been less concerned than ecology with issues of the viability of systems. The question of whether some element in the economy is necessary to or dangerous to the survival of the whole is not a question economists usually ask, but it does have analogues in ecology.

Economists' techniques of evaluation can be illustrated in cases using data on natural ecosystems. George Perkins Marsh described how young trout eat mosquito larvae and then grow up to feed on mayflies. The mayflies that escape the trout in turn eat salmon spawn.

> Hence by a sort of house-that-Jack-built, the destruction of the mosquito that feeds the trout, that preys on the mayfly, that destroys the eggs that hatch the salmon that pampers the epicure, may occasion a scarcity of this latter fish in an area where he would otherwise be abundant. Thus all nature is linked together by invisible bonds . . .[8]

An economist, looking at Marsh's example, would say the ecologist has shown that trout fishermen and salmon fishing are competitive. If too many trout are caught, the mayfly will destroy the salmon. For example, the economist and ecologist, working together, may find that each two trout caught reduces the number of salmon caught by one. Similarly, mosquito control may be competitive with both kinds of fishing. A five percent reduction in mosquito bites may cause a ten percent reduction in the available catch of both fish. In such a case,

[8] Marsh, op. cit., p. 96.

21

the economist may try to determine whether mosquito control or increased or decreased amounts of trout fishing are economically justifiable.

The techniques used for the evaluation are derived from the economists' treatment of equilibrium. The evaluator tries to determine the total benefits and total costs of different levels of activity. The benefits of trout fishing might be measured by the value of trout to its consumers; the costs, by the worth of salmon. The benefits of mosquito control, in terms of reduced itching and disease, might be compared with the costs to all fish eaters. The measures in both cases may be given by market prices, estimated by consumer surveys, or guessed by other techniques. In Fig. 1–4, the benefits and costs of different levels of activity are represented as the total benefit TB and total cost TC curves. Both are drawn under assumptions of diminishing returns.

A well-designed policy or institution is declared to be one that gives the maximum excess of benefits over costs. The economist finds this point either by measuring where the total curves are furthest apart (and hence parallel) or by use of marginal cost and marginal benefit curves. These give the effect on total benefits or costs of *one more unit* of activity at each level of activity. The point at which total benefits exceed total costs by the most is the point at which one more unit of activity will increase total costs by as much as it increases total benefits; it is the point Q_e at which the marginal cost MC curve intersects the marginal benefit MB curve.

The comparison of costs and benefits may be used as the basis of policy. If more trout are being caught than is best, the economist can recommend regulation of the trout fishing. In some cases, an economist will recommend the unimpeded action of supply and demand to maximize benefits. The supply curve in a competitive market may often be a marginal cost curve because companies will increase production as long as price is greater than the cost of producing one more unit. A demand curve may represent the marginal benefit of one more item purchased by the consumer at each price. If this is true, then the intersection of supply and demand curves achieved by the market would automatically equate marginal benefits and marginal costs. Often, however, a market will not work this well. Chapters 4 and 5 for example, discuss the case in which some of the costs of producing a good take the form of pollution, rather than money costs to the manufacturer. In this case, the supply curve is not society's real marginal cost curve. Other institutions are required to attain the best level of activity.

Economists are not the only scientists who can recommend action in a case such as that of the fish and mosquitoes. Ecologists might determine what other trout food might replace mosquito larvae or whether the mayfly might be controlled without harming the trout catch. But if these possibilities are to become the basis of policy or action, they must be introduced by humans. The salmon themselves cannot adopt a new technology for destroying mayflies. If other species the trout can eat are not present in a lake, the trout themselves cannot import them when the mosquitoes are removed. The adoption of the ecologists' schemes depends on the economic action of people, and perhaps on the deliberate comparison of costs and benefits using the techniques of economics.

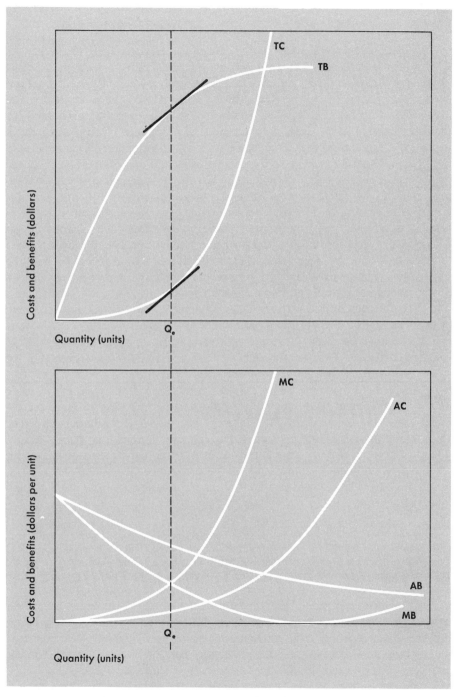

FIG. 1–4 Total, marginal, and average costs and benefits. The TC and TB curves give total dollar values of costs and benefits of different levels of activity (quantity). AC and AB are average costs and benefits (total divided by quantity) at different levels of activity. MC and MB are marginal costs and benefits.

Ecology may use the economists' maximization techniques to discuss the efficiency of natural ecosystems for achieving goals. To do so, however, it must either impose human goals on nature or operate with the assumption that natural species have a simple goal: survival. Survival, though, is an either-or matter, not a question of degree. Ecology has thus been less concerned than economics for the determination of the exact optimum level of production. On the other hand, it has been more concerned than economics with how systems may change or even fail to survive. Concern with marginal costs and benefits may lead economists to miss crucial issues of viability. Markets, or marginal cost calculations, only work to allocate resources efficiently when diminishing returns are perceived as increasing costs. Ecologists argue that by the time certain natural resources reach that point of scarcity, natural ecosystems may already be so disturbed that equilibrium at a level necessary to sustain life or existing social relations may not be obtainable. That critical long-range threshold may be passed by not stopping an activity before short-run costs outweigh benefits is a lesson economists are only now learning from ecology.

Economists' concern with the exact attainment of goals has also led many of them to neglect how the goals themselves are related to society and nature. Another interaction of the economy with nature can illustrate this: the case of commercial forests. Forests with only one kind of pine tree are profitable for paper companies to plant. They allow cheap and massive cutting, and, like many simplified ecosystems, allow a greater population of one plant than a more diversified ecosystem. But "they are wildlife deserts and have no more recreational value than do cornfields."[9] To earn a little money from hunters and convince conservationists they are not destroying other species, the paper companies must bring deer from other forests to be hunted. The benefits of preserving wildlife diversity may be compared with the benefits of increased paper use (as, for disposable evening gowns and tuxedos) or the cost savings from not bothering to recycle newsprint.

> If the *New York Times* were de-inked and recycled instead of being burned that would save nearly 36 square miles of mature Canadian forest each year. Add just a few more cities on the east coast in this recycling plan, and we would save something close to a national park's worth of standing timber a year.[10]

Economists can make this comparison of benefits to recommend national policy. They may also devise institutions that would facilitate these policies. But they might not make the attempt were it not for ecologists. The comparison of costs and benefits and the insistence that tradeoffs between different

[9] Malcolm Margolin, "Forests: The Habit of Waste," *The Nation*, Vol. 210, No. 8, March 2, 1970, pp. 238–40.
[10] *Ibid.*

goals are imposed by nature are the central points made in many textbooks. That costs and benefits may and must be compared is an important lesson. In teaching it, however, economists may neglect the wider context of social structures and natural systems, within which benefits and costs must be measured and specific institutions for conservation or pollution control must be devised. Thus, they may simply take the prices of paper and the amount people are willing to pay for recreation as given, without considering what in society makes paper so much in demand (must government agencies file so much in triplicate?) or makes people so short of time for leisure activities. They may take technology for granted, when technology is in fact mostly developed by paper companies to promote wood use and forest services do not have equivalent capacity to produce wood-saving techniques. To compare the costs and benefits of additional lumbering under those circumstances may be to overlook the forest for the trees. Putting both cost-benefit comparisons and the explanation of changes that do occur in the context of wider choices of systems is something the economist can learn from ecology.

SUMMARY

There are both important similarities and differences between the disciplines of economics and ecology. The description of systems of cause and effect are central to both. The consideration of flow, equilibrium, and change is central to the description of systems in either case. Economics and ecology both study flows (of resources and products; of energy and nutrients) through the systems they describe. Both study the equilibrating mechanisms by which the flows are brought into balance. Both consider the growth and evolution of their respective systems. The two sciences, however, differ in one important matter of emphasis. The systems that economists consider reflect directly the consequences of deliberate human decisions—both in the determination of actions within the systems and in the choice of the basic institutions of the systems themselves. This makes economics appear, at times, to be the study of choice, or *the allocation of scarce resources among competing ends*. But it is also the study of different economic institutions and their effect on behavior and choice. Ecology has been less concerned with deliberate choice, but it has directed its attention to issues of survival often ignored by economics.

Selected Readings

An introduction to economic concepts is found in other books in this series. See particularly Robert Dorfman, *Prices and Markets*, and Gregory Grossman, *Economic Systems*. Ecology is introduced in Edward J. Kormondy, *Concepts of Ecology* (Englewood Cliffs, N. J.: Prentice-Hall, Inc., 1969); and E. P. Odum, *Fundamentals of Ecology* (Philadelphia: W. B. Saunders Co., 1959). Farley Mowat, *Never Cry Wolf* (New York: Dell, 1963) is an enjoyable description of a naturalist's relations to one ecosystem. William H. Miernyk, *The Elements of Input-Output Analysis* (New York: Random House, 1969), is a good introduction to that technique; and Robert M. Solow, *Growth Theory* (New York: Oxford University Press, 1970), introduces simplified mathematical models of economic growth. On the evolution of economic systems, in relation to technology and the environment, see V. Gordon Childe, *Man Makes Himself* (New York: New American Library, 1951), and Maurice Dobb, *Studies in the Development of Capitalism* (New York: International Publishers, 1947). William L. Thomas, ed., *Man's Role in Changing the Face of the Earth* (Chicago: University of Chicago Press, 1956), is an important collection of articles on the effect of economy and society upon the environment.

Population-
Resource Balance

CHAPTER TWO

The principles of economics and ecology have now been introduced. The aim of this book is to apply these principles in considering how economies relate to the environment. Subsequent chapters will consider the problems of pollution and resource conservation, which have become important in developed nations. First, however, an older problem than that of pollution will be considered. The supply of food for subsistence was a practical problem for ancient societies and primitive tribes. It formed the basis for the questions that Malthus and Ricardo asked in the early days of economic science. It is still a pressing concern for many less-developed countries. How food supplies and population interact is the concern of this chapter; how different agricultural institutions may affect the balance will be discussed in Chapter 3.

POPULATION GROWTH AND PRESSURE

Humans, like other species, require nutrition to survive. Particularly when undernourished, they are subject to disease. The natural forces that control animal populations can also limit human populations. When food is abundant, numbers may grow, until food is again scarce. The classical economists assumed this was inevitable. Malthus held that if a people lived at a standard of living above starvation, or as he called it, "misery," they would increase their numbers. Malthus posited a growth rate that would double a population every twenty-five years. On the other hand, he doubted that food production could increase at more than an arithmetic rate. A certain number of tons per

27

year could be added to production, but production would not multiply at a geometric rate each year like population. Eventually there would be too many people for the food available. The natural state of any economy had to be "misery."

Many economists have agreed with Malthus. Others, however, argue that human societies can change the rules by which their economies operate. They can organize their farms and their agricultural research to increase food supply more rapidly than Malthus expected. Perhaps, too, they can reduce their rate of population growth. The results need not be the ones Malthus expected.

Two Possible Models

Economists or ecologists can analyze either of these possibilities as a system of cause and effect relationships. The two possibilities are shown in Figs. 2–1 and 2–2. In each, the horizontal axis shows different levels of per capita food production. The vertical dimension gives different rates of growth per year of food production (G_f) and of population (G_p). If food production grows faster than population, then per capita food production increases. The next year, the economy will be further to the right in the graph. If population grows more rapidly than food supply, per capita availability falls. The economy moves further to the left in the graph. The broken arrows show the direction of change.

In the "Malthusian" economy of Fig. 2–1, the population growth rate is constant at any level of per capita food supply above subsistence. The rate of growth of food supply falls at higher levels of production. Population grows more rapidly than food supply; per capita consumption is driven back to subsistence. In Fig. 2–2, although food production grows at a constant percentage

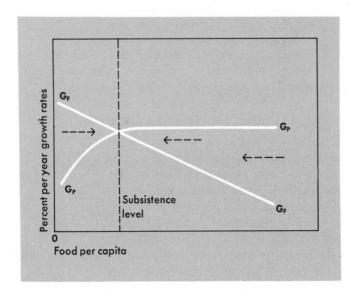

FIG. 2–1 A Malthusian system.

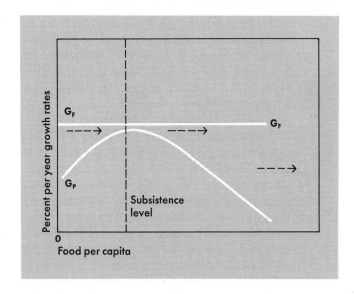

FIG. 2-2 A system with un-limited growth.

rate, population growth slows down at higher consumption levels. In this case, per capita food supply can grow continuously.

Many debates have occurred about which of these patterns of cause and effect is most likely to operate. History shows some populations have declined. Economists have investigated whether food supplies were to blame. One example shows how a Malthusian crisis might come about and also how this ecological calamity affected the rest of the economy.

An Economic Detective Story

The Black Death struck England in 1348. The disease may have been introduced by returning Crusaders. According to contemporary accounts, it decimated the population. Its extent and the reasons for its devastation, however, remained a mystery to historians. Britain, at the time, did not take regular censuses, but a count in 1377 showed population roughly comparable to that enumerated after the Norman Conquest of 1066. The population had presumably increased until the plague and then diminished; no statistics gave the extent of this rise and fall. It took a remarkable piece of historical detection to unravel the record.

The detective was an economic historian, Michael Postan[1]. He used Sherlock Holmes' method of deduction from known facts and established principles to solve the mystery. The principles were taken from economics. The known facts were records of prices and wages paid by monasteries. Unlike total popu-

[1] M. Postan, "Some Economic Evidence of Declining Population in the Later Middle Ages," *Economic History Review* Vol. 2, No. 3, 1950, pp. 221-45.

lation counts, those figures were considered reliable. Postan reasoned that if population decreased, labor would become scarcer than before the plague. Given a fixed amount of land, scarcer labor would receive higher real wages. Postan found that between 1300 and 1425, the purchasing power of a day's wages, measured in wheat, more than doubled. This would seem to indicate the ratio of men to land had fallen, but like a good sleuth, Postan had to rule out other possible explanations for the change.

What else might explain higher farm wages? A technological change in agriculture might have made society better off; workers might have shared in the benefits along with estate owners. Peasants might have fled to the towns, creating a labor shortage only in the countryside. Either effect would have left different price records. Had landowners benefited from general productivity increases, the prices of luxuries they bought would have risen; wheat prices would also have fallen if productivity had risen. Neither effect occurred. The price of wheat rose more than that of some major luxuries. The price that rose most was that of butter, a minor luxury that agricultural laborers with increasing incomes might begin to consume. So, prices were inconsistent with a hypothesis of productivity increase. Records also showed that the few industries in the towns had not expanded much. Migration to towns would have created excess labor supply there, and depressed workers' wages. Because these wages rose in the same way as those in agriculture, migration was eliminated.

Postan thus concluded that the laboring population of England had declined greatly in the fourteenth century. Then, he discovered something that had not been suspected. Postan had expected the price and wage trends to have started suddenly at the time of the Black Death. He found, however, that the trend had started a quarter century before the Black Death. Postan concluded population had been decreasing for a generation before the Black Death, which merely accelerated the decline. This, he reasoned, might have occurred because rapid population growth during the twelfth and thirteenth centuries led the English to bring more land into farms. They had plowed fields not really well suited for cultivation. These farms could yield crops but not for long. After a few years, food had grown scarce. Increased infant mortality, and, eventually, a declining adult population resulted. The Black Death was so devastating because the population was already undernourished.

Storybook detectives usually find direct evidence easier to find once they have deduced the truth indirectly. Once Postan had produced his explanation, his students looked for areas where agriculture had expanded in the thirteenth century. Sure enough, many of the parishes founded then were in parts of England where today only grazing is possible, because soils are not very good. Those parishes had not remained settled for long.

Other Instances of Decline

Fourteenth-century England was not the only country in which population declined after apparently exceeding the ecological basis of its subsistence.

Nineteenth-century Ireland was another. The potato was native to South America and was introduced into Europe by the Spanish. By the eighteenth century, it was known that potato cultivation yielded more food energy from an acre of farmland than wheat or barley. The Irish peasants were already living crowded onto small farms. With the introduction of the potato, these farms could provide more food. Population expanded. In the 1840s, a blight struck the potato plants. Fungicides to control blight had not yet been invented. A large proportion of the population died, and another large portion emigrated in distress.

Sometimes, entire societies disappeared. Ancient Near Eastern civilizations cultivated lands that are deserts today. Some scientists blame wars for laying waste the land, but some believe these were irrigated lands that became saturated with salt because of the irrigation or that they dried out because of deforestation. A similar fate may have befallen the Maya empire. Central American Indians subsisted on the basis of "slash-and-burn" agriculture. Under this system, farmers cut down a small section of tropical forest. They burn the cut trees and brush to restore to the topsoil the nutrients that have been in the plants. Immediately after burning, corn and other crops can grow abundantly on the cleared soil. If cultivation continues for several years, however, the topsoil is depleted. Nutrients are leached out by the rains, and the land becomes useless. To survive, slash and burn farmers must abandon their clearings to regrowth as natural forest and move to new parts of the jungle. According to some archaeologists, the Maya sustained large ceremonial cities by having enough farmers circulating in the surrounding area so that they could send a surplus of food to sustain the priests in the city. They argue soils were reused too often and became depleted. The population either died or dispersed into the jungle; the temples were left abandoned.

Population pressure on food supplies causes severe economic difficulties short of famine. In poor countries, when food supply lags behind demand, the result may be a general inflation that disrupts the rest of the economy.[2] Imports of food to meet the demand seriously affect the balance of payments and make development plans impossible to fulfill. Local famines still occur when wars or disorganized distribution systems prevent the shipment of grain from areas of surplus. The causes of famines are a matter of debate. Some scientists blame wars or social evils, rather than absolute numbers, even for past famines; others argue that population growth will eventually lead to a worldwide famine.

PREVENTIVE AND POSITIVE CHECKS

Stability with Inequality

Population may grow beyond the limit at which food supply will sustain numbers. But must it? Even Malthus admitted that the rate of population growth

31

[2] Matthew Edel, *Food Supply and Inflation in Latin America* (New York: Praeger, 1969).

was not given by nature alone. "Preventive checks," or restraints, to the birth rate might be an alternative to the "positive checks" of famine and epidemic. According to Malthus, individual preventive checks included vice (dissipation, instead of marital relationships) or virtuous abstinence. At the level of the whole society, inequality of income might affect population growth.

Malthus thought the poor only wanted to feed their children, and not to educate them to rise in the world. Thus, if the poor lived above the subsistence level, they would increase their numbers greatly. The rich, too, would have many children if they could see no problem about expanding their fortunes. As Malthus put it:

> I think it will be allowed that no state has hitherto existed where the manners were so simple and the means of subsistence so abundant that no check whatever has existed to early marriage; among the lower classes from the fear of not providing well for their families, or among the higher classes from the fear of lowering their condition in life.[3]

To take from the rich and give to the poor might lead the wealthy to marry later and have fewer children. However, if this lifted the poor above the subsistence level, it would lead them to have more children. They would increase their numbers to the point at which misery would again prevail. Thus, equality, and even charity, would only give misery more company.

Malthus' contemporary, David Ricardo, had a somewhat similar view that divided the rich into capitalists and landlords. When population increased, landlords would benefit from rising rents. Profits would fall, and wages be driven back to the subsistence level. If landlords got to waste a larger share of production, the poor would reach starvation sooner, and population growth would be checked. Both the Black Death and the potato famine may have been provoked, in part, by landed institutions of the sort Ricardo depicted. Medieval English population may have been forced onto areas with poor soil because better parts of England were kept out of cultivation by the nobility. The plagues caused higher death rates among the peasants than among the nobility and clergy. The potato famine also may have occurred because landlords kept part of Ireland from feeding the Irish. Even during the worst years of blight, Ireland might have had agricultural resources enough to feed its population. However, when grain was grown, it was shipped by colonial landlords to England where the charities were able to return only a small portion of the food.

Even the biological aspects of the blight were influenced by the landed institutions. Because so much land was in English estates, most peasants had to plant their entire farms in potatoes. Because the potato was an imported crop, the plants were all genetically similar (which would not have been true in Peru, where the potato originated). With many genetically similar plants crowded together, an epidemic could spread very rapidly. Biological theory would consider

[3] T. R. Malthus, *An Essay on the Principle of Population* (Baltimore: Penguin, 1970).

the virulence of the blight, once it started, as "highly probable." However, the conditions that made it probable were economic.

Stability without Inequality

Inequality, as envisioned by Ricardo and Malthus, can reduce population growth, but it is not the only economic arrangement that can do the job. Other institutions, relying less on starvation, may have a similar effect. Equality can be compatible with a stable population.

The Tsembaga of New Guinea have such an economy. This primitive tribe lives in an isolated jungle. The technological basis of their subsistence is slash-and-burn agriculture. Unlike the Maya, the tribes of New Guinea have apparently maintained this system without overcultivating the land. Anthropologist Roy Rappaport has described the mechanism that keeps Tsembaga population and land use in equilibrium.[4] This mechanism is both an economic and a religious system. It works as a self-regulating system, like many in natural ecology, to keep man and land in balance. New Guinea tribes combine slash-and-burn agriculture with the raising of pigs. The pigs can serve as an emergency store of food because yams and taro, the starchy roots cultivated as food staples, cannot be stored. Pig raising ensures that a brief crop failure will not wipe out the population.

Rappaport also argues the pigs help the Tsembaga prevent overuse and erosion of land and overpopulation. As tribes migrate, families bring their pigs with them. When pigs are scarce, they can be penned up and fed leftovers. As the pig population multiplies, the only way to feed pigs is to let them wander in the forest. If farms are too close together, pigs may damage neighbors' taro patches. This gives families an incentive to keep clearings far enough apart that when they are abandoned, the jungle can regrow quickly. Even so, the number of pigs becomes great enough to be a nuisance every ten or fifteen years. That is the sign that it is time for a ritual pig feast to which the tribe invites other tribes from a considerable distance. This feast brings the pig population back into limits.

The feast also serves other ecological functions. It allows the arrangement of marriages between tribes. This prevents inbreeding, which can be a genetic problem in small, isolated communities. Pig feasts also allow a tribe, in the Tsembaga religion, to "repay debts to their ancestors." These religious obligations are incurred in several activities, including wars with other tribes. When there are too many debts, nobody can start a war. After a pig feast, the slate is clean, and for a couple of years, fighting is again possible. Whether a tribe will fight its neighbors then will depend on whether there are accumulated grievances. The most common cause of hostility is bitterness if pigs have been destroying the other tribe's gardens. If tribes live too close together, or if they have too

[4] Roy A. Rappaport, *Pigs for the Ancestors* (New Haven: Yale University Press, 1967), *passim*.

many people for their land, pigs are more likely to have to fend for themselves in surrounding areas; these ecological pressures thus make war more probable. Overpopulation may also shorten the time until pigs create a problem for farming. Tribes would then decide to have pig feasts after briefer intervals, and wars would be legitimate more often.

Wars with Tsembaga weapons do not kill many people, but a few deaths may be enough to keep population small. What is more, in Tsembaga religion, a state of war requires a taboo on sexual activity, so frequent wars may reduce the birth rate. Finally, avoiding wars may give tribes an incentive not to live too close to other tribes, and a tribe defeated in war may take that as an indication to retreat to a less inhabited region.

The social organization of the Tsembaga and their neighbors thus can serve as a check on population pressure on land. Although these mechanisms may not be strong enough to withstand pressures that contact with European traders and technology will bring to New Guinea, they seem to have worked under conditions of primitive technology and isolation. In this case, at least, checks to population occurred with no starvation, and with only a little fighting. Whether similar mechanisms can exist at other levels of economic development is an important concern for economists.

DEVELOPMENT AND POPULATION

The level and rate of growth of income is itself one of the main influences on population growth. Several trends in birth rates and death rates have been associated with increasing per capita production. In preindustrial societies, population growth rates have been low. A birth rate of thirty or thirty-five offspring per year for each thousand inhabitants might be matched by a death rate of thirty per thousand, leaving a growth rate of population of five per thousand (0.5 percent).

Industrialization and improved medical and agricultural technologies in Europe, beginning in the seventeenth century, led to a sharp drop in the death rate, particularly due to a decline in infant mortality. Birth rates also increased slightly, perhaps due to a greater affluence and maternal health, perhaps merely because decreased infant mortality increased the proportion of women of child-bearing age in the population. The result was an increase in the overall population growth rate to close to 2 percent per year. In latter-day less-developed countries, where public health care and new technologies were introduced from abroad and death rates fell more rapidly, population growth was even faster. While birth rates rose to more than forty per thousand annually, death rates fell as low as ten per thousand. Population growth rates in Latin America exceed three percent per year. In such a circumstance, population will double in slightly less than the twenty-five years that terrified Malthus.

In the industrialized nations of Europe, North America, and Japan, however, birth rates had begun to fall by the time the death rate fell below twenty per thousand. Where death rates reached ten per thousand, birth rates were approximately twenty per thousand. One percent annual population growth rates are common; in a few European countries, birth rates have fallen so much that zero population growth has resulted (except for the arrival of immigrants).

Several factors contribute to the decline in birth rates. The decline of peasant farming and of child labor in factories removed the need to rely on children's efforts to supplement family income. Employment for women outside the home may also reduce family size. The increasing importance of education also slows population growth. The requirement of schooling before young people can obtain jobs will discourage having children, in two ways. First, people may delay childbearing until they have completed their own education. Second, the high cost of educating one's own children deters parents from having large families. Increased incomes and higher levels of education also allow wider communication of effective family planning technologies to take place. Better living standards, social security, and the very fact of lower death rates made parents less dependent on having many children to ensure having someone to support them in their old age.

Increased per capita income may also stimulate higher birth rates. As Malthus suggested, wealthier families may feel more confident of their ability to provide for more children. If developed and less-developed countries are considered separately, countries with higher incomes have slightly higher rates of population growth within each category. Some economists suggest, in the light of the American "baby boom" that followed the depression and World War Two, that high-income families consider children "luxuries" whose "consumption" can be increased. Others suggest that larger families would be attractive only to a generation that received an increase in income over the level of wealth its parents knew.[5] In this case, an increase in living standards followed by stabilization at the higher income level would cause only a temporary increase in the rate of population growth. Whether the decline in birth rates in the United States in the 1960s was due to this, to new birth-control technologies, or to attitude changes like women's liberation is not known. Economists have not been notably successful at predicting short-term changes in population growth. Only the difference in relative rates of growth between developed and less-developed areas stands as an established generalization.

The Low-level Equilibrium Trap

Because population growth rates decline with economic development, development might seem to be an automatic mechanism for controlling the size of populations. Like the predator-prey relationship of Townshend's dogs and goats or like the ritual cycle of the Tsembaga, industrialization might be seen as work-

35

[5] Richard A. Easterlin, "Population," in *Contemporary Economic Issues*, ed. N. W. Chamberlain (Homewood, Ill.: Richard D. Irwin Inc., 1969), pp. 241–72.

ing automatically to keep populations within limits. However, economic development does not seem to work that well as an automatic mechanism for population control, because if population pressure on land is too great or population growth rates are too high, development itself is more difficult.

Demographic pressure complicates the task of developing an economy in many ways. More of the society's effort must go to food production, leaving fewer economic resources for developing industry. If nutrition is inadequate, even after this agricultural effort, the productive ability of the population may suffer. A faster increase of the labor force requires that a large part of each year's savings be spent in merely equipping each new worker with as much machinery as other workers have on the average. Little is left over for increasing the amount of capital per worker. A high birth rate (even if matched by a high death rate in a poor country with zero population growth) leads to an age composition of the population with a large proportion too young to work. A higher ratio of consumers to workers and a need to feed and educate many children, some of whom will not survive to working age, can also cut into the development effort.

As a result, rapid population growth may prevent the economic development that would otherwise be the "cure" for the demographic change. Instead of moving to a position of high incomes with low rates of population growth, an economy may stagnate, with increases in population absorbing all increases in production. This possibility was analyzed as a system of causes and effects in Fig. 2–1. This system, however, fails to show that if incomes become sufficiently high, then population increase will slow down and growth continue indefinitely, as in Fig. 2–2.

A system under which either possibility can occur is presented in Fig. 2–3. As in the previous figures, levels of production per capita are represented by the horizontal axis; rates of growth on the vertical axis. Population growth rates (G_p) are assumed to increase at income levels above subsistence, as they do in the early stages of economic development. At per capita production levels (including food and other production) above some level $A, they begin to fall. Meanwhile, the growth rate of production (G_y) is assumed to be greater at higher levels of per capita production than at lower levels because higher incomes allow more expenditure on equipment, research, education, and other investments that can accelerate growth.

As in the previous figures, the broken arrows represent the direction in which per capita production will change, at any level. At levels between subsistence and $B per capita, the rate of growth of population exceeds that of production. The system is driven back to subsistence. If, however, production can once exceed $B per capita, total production will grow faster than population. The economy will grow perpetually, and population growth rates will continue to fall.

Economists call this situation a "low-level equilibrium trap."[6] It will have

[6] Richard R. Nelson, "A Theory of the Low-Level Equilibrium Trap," *American Economic Review*, December 1956, pp. 894–08.

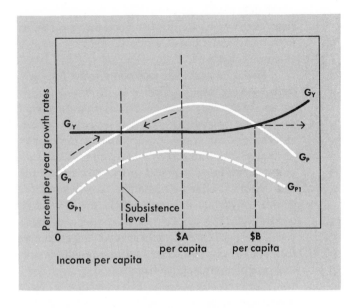

FIG. 2–3 Low-level equilibrium trap.

a stable equilibrium position at the subsistence level, which can be broken only if the economy can raise income beyond $B. This trap is sometimes presented as a law of nature, from which less-developed nations cannot escape, except perhaps with a large boost from foreign aid or investment to lift their income beyond $B. There are, however, other possibilities that do not rely on the automatic working of the economic mechanism. Deliberate economic policies may raise the rate of economic growth at any level of income per head, or lower the rate of population growth.

Population Planning

The advantages of a reduced birth rate for development can be illustrated using Fig. 2–3. If family planning programs could cut the rate of population growth at different income levels, the dotted curve G_{p1} might replace the original G_p curve. Because this curve is below the G_y curve, there would be no low-level equilibrium trap. Per capita production would grow continuously. For this reason, many economists propose that less-developed countries direct resources into population planning.

These programs are controversial. Some experts argue that social customs in some societies lead people to want large families. They think that to change people's ideas and lead them to want fewer children will require an expensive effort at changing public opinion. Difficulties encountered by some government programs to promote birth control in India and other less-developed countries are cited to support their arguments. If population programs are expensive, then they will reduce the resources available for other development programs. This

37

could shift the G_y curve in Fig. 2–3 even lower, and make the low-level equilibrium trap worse. Sometimes, however, even expensive programs are considered to be worthwhile because it is thought they will lower the G_p by more than the G_y curve is lowered.

Social custom will not necessarily prevent population planning programs from working. Higher birth rates in less-developed than in developed countries do not necessarily stem from different fundamental values. Some institutions, such as the absence of effective programs of social security or the presence of child labor, may create an incentive to have many children. These incentives act on motives for increased living standards and security in old age that are not particular to less-developed areas. When these insecurities are removed, population growth declines. Population growth rates fell in Taiwan when GNP began to rise. In mainland China, where the communist economy guarantees income to the elderly, birth control has spread despite low per capita income. Even given these incentives, poor people might not want families much larger than those of the more affluent, but they might be unable to limit their families due to a lack of contraceptive technologies.

There is considerable evidence that a desire for birth control technologies is widespread even in traditional or poor societies. Anthropologists report that many primitive peoples attempt to practice birth control through the use of primitive remedies. In Latin America, surveys in several cities showed that, despite religious opposition, abortions were common. However, adequate contraception, like any technology, cannot be used unless methods are learned and the equipment required is available. Not only are newer methods of birth control (pills to prevent ovulation, intrauterine devices, vasectomy) often unknown in poor countries, but older methods (calculation of the rhythm of fertility, condoms, diaphragms) may not be sufficiently known for effective use. The scarcity of reliable birth control information (and devices) among the poor is, in part, simply a result of limited income and education, which make the acquistion of any information and equipment difficult.

Population planning would be economically feasible if lack of social security and information were the main reasons for its absence. Its moral and political desirability is, however, often questioned. Some religions hold family planning, except by abstention, to be immoral. Birth control programs have also been criticized as efforts to limit the freedom of the world's poor. The motivation for these programs is claimed to be the reduction of the number of poor or nonwhite people, to reduce the threat of revolution directed against rich or white people.

Advocates of birth control programs often lend credence to these charges, when they evoke fear of teeming hordes of poor nonwhite natives. United States economists, in trying to apply economic calculation to problems of development, have restated the low-level equilibrium trap argument in terms of the worth of individuals. Instead of holding that population pressure is a problem for the system, they say the economic value of each individual born in less-developed areas may be negative. This restatement is imprecise as economics because it only considers the individuals worthwhile as machines for producing more food than they consume and not as having other values to others and to themselves. Naturally, it is also offensive to members of racial minorities in the United States and to people in poor countries.

But need programs to promote family planning be manipulative? One stereotype is that middle class people and residents of rich countries want small families, but that the poor and people in preindustrial countries want many children. If the different birth rates resulted from fundamental differences in groups' values, to try to change these desires directly would be manipulation. If, however, poor people have wanted birth control information all along, reliable information and equipment, whatever its sources, can be useful to them. Even if the motives of population planners are as bad as their opponents suggest, these programs need not manipulate and victimize poor people or countries, as long as they rely on voluntary compliance.

Some writers even suggest that the wealthy and powerful have traditionally kept birth control information from the poor. Although knowledge and goods are scarce in less-developed countries, private advertisers and government agencies provide poor people with information and devices for some purposes. They introduced transistor radios and mosquito control, which increased population by limiting malaria. Until recently, they did not do so with birth control technologies. Economic analysis of benefits and costs may give an explanation.

Holders of wealth may have an incentive to acquire information on birth control for their own use. If they view the rest of the population basically as employees or tenants, however, capitalists and landlords may have an economic incentive not to spread information to the poor that will limit their numbers. A greater population growth rate among the nonowners of land or capital in a society may bid rents or profits upwards. Professor Postan's detective deductions were based on this fact. The effect of family planning would be similar to that of population reduction by plagues: wages would rise. Arguments about profits and wages are commonly used in debates about immigration, which has the same effect on wages as high birth rates. Although these arguments have not been used much in debates about birth control, population growth rates may be biased upward if enlightened self-interest leads employers to support health measures that increase the supply of workers, but to ignore support for family planning.[7]

Recent support by charitable foundations and conservative governments for population control may result from fear that revolution would be more costly than higher wages. Perhaps the concern is simply that poor countries be helped to overcome the low-level equilibrium trap. In either event, however, more reliable institutional devices than philanthropy can be imagined for the limitation

[7] Herman E. Daly, "The Population Question in Northeastern Brazil," *Economic Development and Cultural Change* Vol. 18, No. 4, July 1970, pp. 536–74.

of birth rates. Greater equality in society, if it made education and security more widespread, could lead to greater and more effective use of birth control technologies. Greater freedom, especially for women, could have a similar effect.

SUMMARY

Population growth was the first ecological problem to concern economists. The balance between population and food supply illustrates the relation between the economy and the environment, and the use of economists' techniques of analysis. It is also important for economic policy. Malthus, and other classical economists, argued that prosperity would affect population growth. Increasing population would drive any economy back to a subsistence level. This chapter shows that in some societies, population growth did lead to famine or plague. Thirteenth-century England and nineteenth-century Ireland are examples. Other societies are organized so excessive population growth is avoided. The Tsembaga of New Guinea are an example of this. A system may operate in a way opposite to that assumed by Malthus; reducing poverty may reduce, rather than increase, population growth. Recent history of the developed nations indicates this prediction may be better than that of Malthus' "dismal science." The model of the "low-level equilibrium trap" suggests that this may be true at higher income levels even if population growth would drive incomes to the subsistence level if they began below a critical level of poverty. Population planning programs are often urged for countries faced with this trap, but even for these countries greater equality of social security may help promote small families.

Selected Readings

Carlo M. Cipolla, *The Economic History of World Population* (Baltimore: Penguin Books, 1962), is a basic reference. Paul R. Ehrlich and Anne H. Ehrlich, *Population, Resources, Environment* (San Francisco: W. H. Freeman and Co., 1970), includes an introduction to demographic principles and a Malthusian description of the current world. Malthus' *First Essay on Population* is available in several editions, and Ronald L. Meek, ed., *Marx and Engels on the Population Bomb* (Berkeley, Cal.: Ramparts Press, 1971), presents critiques of the Malthusians. Frank W. Notestein, "The Population Crisis: Reasons for Hope," *Foreign Affairs,* (October 1967), pp. 167–80, reviews recent population control programs. Cecil Woodham-Smith, *The Great Hunger* (New York: Harper and Row, 1962), is an excellent history of the Irish famine; Josue DeCastro, *The Black Book of Hunger* (New York: Funk and Wagnalls, 1967), discusses famine and malnutrition in the current world. Richard A. Easterlin, "Population," in Neil W. Chamberlain, *Contemporary Economic Issues* (Homewood, Ill.: Richard D. Irwin Inc., 1969), pp. 241–72, is a good introduction to economists' measurements of factors affecting birth rates.

Institutions

and Food Supply

CHAPTER THREE

Balance between population and food supply is maintained by more than birth and death rates. Economic systems also affect this balance by altering society's use of natural resources in agriculture, fishing, hunting, and live-stock raising. Because low population growth rates are most likely if incomes are high, the performance of food producing industries during economic development is crucial for the eventual stabilization of population at adequate standards of living.

This chapter discusses the potential of world agriculture. Feeding a world population larger than the present 3.5 billion is technically possible, and modern agricultural technology may allow countries to escape the low-level equilibrium trap. This, however, will require adequate economic institutions. A few of the many possible institutional arrangements are discussed. Some affect the efficiency of individual producing units, others act on the rate of reinvestment of the economy as a whole. A comparison of the economic histories of Japan and Java illustrates some of the potentials and the dangers. One institutional pitfall discussed, the overuse of common resources, is also of interest because of similarities to the causes of pollution discussed in later chapters.

THE POTENTIAL OF AGRICULTURE

Malthusian literature often depicts world population as growing until there is literally no room to stand. A more realistic fear is exhaustion of food supplies. However, world population as a whole is probably not yet near this limit. Edward J. Kormondy has calculated that if all of the solar energy utilized by present ecosystems were used exclusively for human food production, the maximum possible world population would be 600 billion people.[1] This would require that man be exclusively a herbivore; that there be no other animals to eat vegetable products; and that the food used include all of the plant production of the oceans as well as land areas. If diets are assumed to require meat as well, the limit would be 30 to 60 billion people, because of the energy loss through consumption by the other herbivores which then would be utilized for meat.

Kormondy cautions, however, that the assumption of perfectly efficient capture of energy for human use involves "outright prevarications of the natural scene . . . Such speculations and predictions are a kind of scientific fun [and] lead back to fundamental principles . . . though their conclusions have little comfort for the scientist as humanist."[2] More immediate barriers to human food availability are imposed by limits to the capacities of current domesticated plants and animals as energy converters, by the competition they receive from other species, and by local limits to the availability of water and mineral nutrients. Whether these barriers would limit human population to twice its current numbers, or to three, four, or more times that many, is uncertain. Even though sustenance of the present population is within the capacity of current production technologies, regional famines still occur because productive capacity and growing populations are located in different places. Increasing food production, at least in some places, is necessary to meet immediate needs as well as to accommodate future population growth.

The observation, discussed in the last chapter, that birth rates fall in the course of economic development, points up the need for expanding food production in the near future. If income throughout the world could be raised to the level of one or two thousand dollars per capita, historical experience indicates that near-zero population growth would be feasible. This could allow the attainment of an equilibrium between population and resources at a high standard of living. If population growth must eventually be limited by rising death rates at low income, an equilibrium between population and resources is also inevitable, but it will be one of world poverty, malnutrition, and short life spans.

The "Green Revolution"

The problem for less-developed countries may be depicted as the low-level equilibrium trap, using the diagram introduced in the previous chapter. Fig. 3–1, however, is drawn to show population growth rates (G_p) falling to zero at high levels of income. The initial relation of food production growth rates (G_{F1}) is drawn to intersect the G_p curve twice; at any level of income below B (perhaps $900 per capita), the economy will be driven back to the subsistance level

---

[1] Edward J. Kormondy, *Concepts of Ecology* (Englewood Cliffs, N. J.: Prentice-Hall, Inc., 1969), p. 177.

[2] *Ibid.*

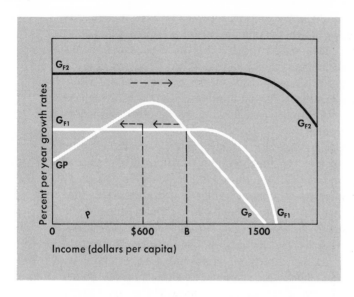

FIG. 3–1 Escaping low-level equilibrium.

of income (probably about $100 per capita). However, if food production growth rates can be increased, as shown by curve G_{F2}, the economy will escape from the low-level trap, even starting out at the subsistence level. Both G_F curves are drawn so that food production growth rates also fall to zero at some point, but the income level involved may depend on population growth rates. With a higher world population, the maximum sustainable per capita production will be low because population growth will have slowed down sooner, and the final equilibrium population will be smaller.

How is agricultural production to be expanded? Although the final level of production is limited by solar energy supplies, the initial impetus to production can use an additional source of energy: the stored-up energy from long-dead life in fossil fuels. Petroleum can be used both as raw material and energy source for the production of nitrogenous fertilizers and, some scientists think, perhaps for the direct feeding of microorganisms. Limited world supplies of petroleum provide a reserve that can be used once in attempting to escape the low-level trap. They allow time both to slow down world population growth and to develop alternatives to petroleum fertilizer for sustained, expanded production. Attempts to increase production can take several forms. Selective breeding and hybridization can improve the ability of plant and animal species to utilize energy and nutrients. Control of pests, weeds, and diseases can increase the extent to which energy and nutrients are captured by edible plants. Investments and new technologies for the preparation and delivery of fertilizer, nutrients, and water to crops, and for the harvest and delivery of products can increase output as well.

44

The most notable recent advance has been the breeding of new plant varieties. Hybrid corn increased United States per-acre production several times over. The development of high yield Mexican wheat and the "miracle rice" of the 1960s produced the so-called Green Revolution in tropical agriculture. These two varieties, which can double production per acre, were developed by breeding plants able to make best use of fertilizer. The application of chemical nutrients and water enables grains to make better use of tropical solar energy and to grow rapidly. However, the plants best adapted to tropical conditions were generally long-stemmed varieties. These could compete successfully with weeds for access to sunlight, and were also adapted to withstanding tropical plant diseases. With fertilization, heavier grain pods and longer stems made them become top-heavy, fall over, and die. New hybrids were developed by crossing the existing tropical varieties with dwarf breeds that had short, thick stems. The short varieties finally developed could withstand both tropical conditions and increased weight.[3]

The Green Revolution has led to some problems, however. The new plants require increased water supplies for growth, as compared with older tropical varieties. The needed irrigation systems are breeding grounds for parasites. The worst is schistosomiasis, a debilitating, and often fatal, disease spread by infested, water dwelling snails. If large areas are planted to a genetically uniform crop variety, pest control also becomes more difficult. Plant diseases, such as the Irish potato blight, become more likely. Because they are shorter, the new plants are also more vulnerable to the competition of weeds. Both weeds and predators become more numerous due to the greater availability of fertilizer nutrients and of ripening grain. The use of chemical pesticides, the simplest initial method for control of predators, has at times led to severe ecological damage.

The most familiar example of this damage involved the use of DDT and other chlorinated hydrocarbon insecticides. These chemicals may be absorbed in water, and then by plants and animals, without undergoing chemical decomposition. They slowly accumulate in the oceans and in the bodies of aquatic animals. They are most dangerous to carnivorous birds, which consume smaller sea animals, which in turn have eaten other waterborne plants or animals. At each stage of such a food chain, the consumer ingests all of the DDT that has been consumed by all of the creatures at lower levels of the food chain. Because each consumer ingests many times its body weight in plants or animals over its lifetime, the DDT concentration in the body of a carnivore is many times that in plants or in the sea itself. Such high DDT concentrations in birds weaken the shells of eggs and the reproduction of eagles, pelicans, and other species then is threatened. The effects of DDT concentrations on other species have not been determined, but the dangers are considered great. Increased crop cultivation made possible by DDT may therefore have a high cost in loss of marine resources.

Other ecological problems may result from insecticide use. Spraying of

45

[3] E. C. Stakman, R. Bradfield, and P. C. Mangelsdorf, *Campaigns Against Hunger* (Cambridge: Harvard University Press, 1967), *passim*.

cocoa groves to destroy cocoa borers in Malaysia proved ineffective for stopping the damage the borers caused, and also increased the numbers of leafhoppers and hopper caterpillars infecting the plants. Further increases in the DDT doses to stem these pests not only failed, it led to an infestation by bagworms. In each case, the insecticides used had done more damage to natural predators which lived off of, and limited, the insect pests than was done to the pests themselves. A similar phenomenon occurred from the spraying of cotton fields to control pests in Peru. In both cases, pest damage was greatly reduced when insecticide spraying was finally ended, and more selective methods of pest control were applied.[4]

Agrarian Institutions and Change

The ecological problems created by side effects of the Green Revolution have led some economists and ecologists to doubt that the new hybrids really will allow an escape from the menace of expanding population. Others, however, have argued that the problems can be avoided if care is taken in the way in which the new technology is applied. This care, though, requires that very well-designed economic institutions be used in carrying out the Green Revolution. The kinds of institutions that are needed have themselves become the focus of controversy. The debate has centered on the relative merits of large commercial farms and systems based on peasant family farming.

The provision of water, fertilizer, and insecticides required for planting the new hybrid grains has often seemed to require large farms as an agricultural institution. Larger farms can both coordinate irrigation systems and the application of other inputs, and can muster the capital or the credit needed to begin production for the first time. Agricultural extension services and the sales departments of private seed and fertilizer companies also are often designed for spreading new techniques among farmers with larger operations. At best, very small farms require a more complex set of institutions, to coordinate their water supplies and to spread information to their owners, than do larger farms. At worst, it is sometimes argued that peasants are disinterested in economic progress. Theories have been developed that claim that peasants are fatalistic, that they do not believe progress to be possible, or that they are unable to make new decisions.

These theories are often challenged.[5] Statistical studies show that in many peasant societies, farmers do respond to incentives by increasing production of goods whose prices rise. Nonetheless, farmers with small farms often do reject innovations. A farmer whose income is not far above bare subsistence is not likely to risk his family's living by adopting a new crop or method, the success

[4] M. T. Farvar and J. Milton, eds., *The Careless Technology* (New York: Natural History Press, 1972), *passim.*

[5] The debate is reviewed in Matthew Edel, "Innovative Supply: A Weak Point in Economic Development Theory," *Social Science Information*, Vol. 9, No. 3, June 1970, pp. 9–40.

of which is uncertain. A commercial farmer with greater assets can afford more risks because devoting part of his land to a new crop, or even a whole year's production if he has resources to sustain himself for longer, is not to put his very life on the line. Developing production of new crops in peasant societies, therefore, may require a system of crop insurance guarantees. These guarantees, plus the difficulty of spreading information to peasants, seem to make family farming an expensive method of agricultural change in less-developed countries.

The ecological critique of the Green Revolution, however, suggests that some advantages of small farms may outweigh the costs.[6] In order to keep down the costs of supervision and labor, large farms generally plant large areas in single crop varieties and use pest control systems, which are cheaply applied over these large areas with little use of labor. The proximity of many identical plants increases the dangers of plant epidemics (or at least requires more insecticide to prevent them). Genetic uniformity limits the pool of varieties available for further breeding experiments, or as a reserve for use if some plague strikes the more common breeds. Smaller farms are more likely to use part-time labor of family members for weeding or localized pesticide application, than to spray from airplanes. They also are more likely to cultivate a variety of crops for their own consumption than are larger farms. This is an argument in favor of governments bearing the cost of supporting and insuring small farmers.

An additional argument holds that unemployment created by introducing the Green Revolution through large commercial farms may frustrate progress. In many areas, the new technology has allowed owners of larger commercial farms to increase their relative profitability advantage over the holders of smaller properties. Often, this has allowed them to increase the size of their farms by buying more land. Owners of other farms may rent to them, rather than to their former tenant families. Although some new jobs are created to provide inputs for agriculture, and in the gathering of the new and larger commercial harvests, the number of unemployed rural workers often rises. So does inequality in the size of farms. Rural unemployment can increase environmental problems in cities by leading to rapid migration to urban areas. Opposition to the increased wealth of large farm owners often leads to political objections to the new technologies, and even to riots to prevent their use.

These considerations suggest that, socially and ecologically, introduction of new technologies to small farms might be the best way to introduce the Green Revolution. A system of institutions will, however, be required to support farm families if they are to improve agriculture. Some of these institutions would be educational services. Widespread literacy and the diffusion of farming information played an important role in the growth of North American agriculture. County agents and schoolteachers paid by the government, as well as private information sources such as Sears Roebuck catalogues, helped to bring about

[6] Clifton R. Wharton, Jr., "The Green Revolution: Cornucopia or Pandora's Box?" *Foreign Affairs*, April 1969; Harry M. Cleaver, Jr., "Contradictions of the Green Revolution," *Monthly Review*, Vol. 24, No. 2, June 1972, pp. 80–111.

this awareness. A system of Folk High Schools helped to pave the way for modernization of peasant agriculture in Denmark. Cooperatives also can help groups of small farms to achieve some of the advantages in production of large farms. These were also important in Denmark and parts of the United States. Other communal institutions also suggest that more can be done to make groups of families more efficient in agriculture. The *kibbutz* and *moshav* in Israel have been very successful. Some reports from China indicate that communes are becoming efficient agricultural producers.[7] If patterns of institutions for the effective spread of technology among small farmers, or communities of small farms, can be developed, the potential of the Green Revolution may be considerably enhanced.

INCENTIVES AND RESOURCE USE

Accessibility to information, and flexibility in adapting to ecological needs are not the only aspects of institutions which affect food production. An economic system must also be designed to give producers incentives to use resources effectively. Chapter 1 described how economists define a well-designed institution as one which assures the maximum excess of benefits over costs. This can be achieved, in some cases, if individual decision makers have incentives to balance the marginal costs and benefits of additional resource use. Some ill-designed institutions give farmers or fishermen larger shares of benefits than they do of costs, leading them to overproduce; other institutions lead these decision makers to produce too little, by giving them smaller shares of the benefits than they bear of the costs. In either case, food production may be reduced.

Overfishing and Common Resources

Ill-designed institutions presently endanger one of the world's important sources of food: the ocean fisheries. In the mid-1960s, approximately 60-million metric tons of fish were caught each year. Ecologists estimate that careful fishing could double that catch, significantly increasing world protein supplies. Maintaining a high fish yield requires that fish not be caught too young, before they reach adequate weight. Enough fish must be left uncaught to breed a new generation. With some species, however, these elementary conservation requirements have not been followed.

Modern technology has allowed major increases in the efficiency of fishing. Sonar and larger nets let fishing fleets capture larger proportions of the fish in an area than was possible in the past. Larger numbers of boats and longer fishing seasons also allow a larger portion of the fish to be caught. Unfortunately,

[7] Eliyahu Kanovsky, *The Economy of the Israeli Kibbutz* (Cambridge, Mass.: Harvard University Press, 1966); Maxwell I. Klayman, *The Moshav in Israel* (New York: Praeger, 1970); Jan Myrdal, *Report from a Chinese Village* (New York: Pantheon, 1965).

when too many of the fish in an area are caught, the size of the population for future years' fishing may be reduced or even extinguished completely. In the 1960s, the herring catch off Britain, Norway, and Iceland first increased, and then declined to almost nothing in a few years. The California sardine harvest had ended even earlier. The catch of some varieties of tuna and shrimp have been reduced in some ocean regions. (Several species of whales are also near extinction from overhunting.)

Why are fish and whales caught in such quantity as to imperil future yields? The reason is that an individual fishing crew has little effective incentive to reduce its catch. It will receive all of the value of its catch, but it will not receive the full benefit of abstaining from catching more. The fish it throws back as too young may be caught by some other boat, not by itself. There is no certainty it will catch the offspring of the fish it lets live to breed. Abstention is wise if the fishermen will share in its rewards, but unless each fisherman is sure every other fisherman will also refrain from catching young fish, or too many fish, he cannot expect much from the future. His best bet is to catch all he can, as fast as he can. Each fisherman will overfish, and all will, taken together.[8]

Overfishing is not inevitable, if fishermen can agree to limit their activities. All may benefit by a uniform reduction in fishing, if they can sign a contract among themselves, or if their governments impose restrictions on them. Limits to the number of days of fishing, the areas in which fishing is allowed, the size of boats, and the mesh of nets can all reduce a catch by reducing the intensity of fishing or allowing smaller fish to slip through uncaught. Agreements and enforcement are difficult to achieve, however, particularly when different nations are competing on the same ocean fishing grounds. Treaties often are signed too late to prevent the destruction of fish resources. Overfishing is not the only threat to marine food resources—pollution is another danger—but overfishing may be part of the reason humanity does not make efficient use of the seas.

Destruction of fish resources because fishermen of different countries have inadequate incentives for conservation, is an example of a problem that is central in many discussions of economics and ecology. The problem is that of the *commons*. From the economic viewpoint, a common is a public resource which individuals may put to private use, as long as they do not exclude others from trying to use it as well. Fisheries are commons. So are the air and some water and waste disposal resources that are discussed in the next two chapters. The problem posed by the common, however, can be seen most simply in its original form. The town park that sometimes survives today under this name is the remnant of communal cow pastures, and even cultivated fields, that existed in precapitalist Europe.

William Forster Lloyd, a contemporary of Malthus, was one of the first

[8] Ralph Turvey, "Optimization and Suboptimization in the Fishing Industry," *American Economic Review*, Vol. 54, No. 2, March 1964, pp. 64–76; George Borgstrom, "The Harvest of the Seas," in Harold W. Helfrich, Jr., *The Environmental Crisis* (New Haven: Yale University Press, 1970), pp. 65–84.

economists to deplore this institution. He asked, "Why are cattle on the common so puny and stunted? Why is the common itself so bareworn and cropped so differently from the adjoining enclosures?" Lloyd looked to incentives to explain the difference.

> The difference depends on the difference in the way in which an increase of stock . . . affects the circumstances of the author of the increase. If a person puts more cattle onto his own field, the amount of the subsistence which they consume is all deducted from the subsistence that was at the command of his original stock. And if before there was no more than a sufficiency of pasture, he reaps no benefit from the additional cattle, what is gained in one way being lost in the other. But if he puts more cattle on a common, the food which they consume forms a deduction which is shared between all the cattle, as well that of others as of his own in proportion to their number, and only a small part of it is taken from his own cattle.[9]

Stated in terms of contemporary economics, we may suppose there is a maximum efficient carrying capacity for a pasture. Adding one more steer will lead to a loss of beef sales from the remaining animals (due to malnutrition) as great as the value of the beef from the new steer. An owner-operator will learn not to add that animal because his marginal cost exceeds his marginal benefit. The user of a common pasture will introduce it, because he will profit by selling the steer, while his neighbor's animals will suffer the loss of food. (He receives the marginal benefit, but bears no marginal cost.) The owner of a pasture who rents to cattlemen also will be able to earn the most if the optimum number of cattle are grazed. If he charges rent that would be reasonable, on a pasture that is not overgrazed, but tries to overgraze the pasture, it will not be profitable for cattle owners to rent from him.

Based on this argument, it has been customary for economists to argue that common resources should be sold to individual operators, or rented out by the government at competitive prices. These are not the only possible responses. A free common might be justified if it allowed poor people to have milk cows for their families. It would have to be regulated carefully to prevent overgrazing and ensure that it was the poor who used it. However, such regulation can achieve the equivalent efficient level of resource use as a price mechanism. As the ocean fisheries show, conservation regulation may be difficult, but it has been achieved for some inland fisheries. Some primitive societies, such as the Tsembaga discussed in Chapter 2, were able to cultivate common resources without overusing them. Institutions other than the market kept each family from growing more than a necessary and viable level of produce. The price mechanism is only one possible mechanism for regulating resource use. In a society in which use of most resources is regulated by prices, however, overuse of a common resource can be a serious problem.

[9] William Forster Lloyd, "Two Lectures on the Checks to Population" (1833) in *Population, Evolution and Birth Control,* ed. Garrett Hardin (San Francisco: W. M. Freeman, 1969), p. 29. See also Garrett Hardin, "The Tragedy of the Commons," *Science,* Vol. 162, 1868, pp. 1243–1248.

Pastures and fisheries are not the only commons that may be overused. The waste-dispersing capacities of air and water may be overtaxed in the same way: the example of the commons has been used to analyze pollution. William Forster Lloyd himself extended the analogy to population growth. He analyzed the common in order to attack poor relief. He argued assistance would lead the poor to have too many children, by freeing parents from the costs of child rearing. This argument has been revived by the biologist, Garrett Hardin. He argues that because population growth puts overall burdens on society, any parent who has children is using some common resources, and should not be allowed to do so in an unregulated way. As a statement that the price system does not automatically regulate population growth by an "invisible hand," this is unobjectionable. As Chapter 2 argues, other mechanisms besides the market may make population a "self-regulating system." Charging a market price for the right to bear offspring may not be the best way to reduce population growth. Lloyd and Hardin do show, however, that there are many other problems which have some analogy to the argument about the common.

Incentives for Underproduction

Institutions may also give producers too little incentive for resource use. This is apparent from a comparison of owner-operated farms with sharecropping. If a farmer owns his farm, performs the labor needed for production, and buys the fertilizer and other inputs, he can compare the costs and benefits of different levels of effort. Because he receives the value of crops produced, he will use more labor or fertilizer, if either input will add more to output than it costs (in dollars or in what the farmer thinks his labor is worth). He will, therefore, produce up to the point at which diminishing returns drive the marginal product of additional effort down to equal the marginal cost. As discussed in the last section of Chapter 1, this is the efficient level.

The situation is different if the farmer is a sharecropper, bound by law or custom to give half of his product to a landlord. If the farmer still must supply all of the labor and other inputs, he will use them only up to the point at which *his share* of the marginal product equals the marginal cost. This will mean working up to the point at which an additional amount of labor or fertilizer will add twice its value to output. If there are diminishing returns, the sharecropper will produce much less on the same sized farm than an owner-operator.

The same difficulties will not arise if the farmer pays a fixed rent for his land. He will still receive the marginal benefit of each unit of inputs or effort in which he invests, and has the incentive to produce up to the point at which benefit equals marginal cost.

Slavery gave the least incentive of any system for effective resource use. The slave received none of the benefit if he increased his productivity. Poor performance of farming tasks, destruction of farm animals, inability to introduce efficient but easily broken tools, and soil exhaustion all are problems which inhibited slave agriculture; all have been interpreted as forms of covert resistance

51

by slaves to the desires of their owners. Thus, even though slave populations often did not have enough children to grow in numbers, they were not ecologically viable because production decreased.

Slavery and fixed-proportion sharecropping are not the only inefficient institutional systems possible in agriculture; nor are cash rentals and owner occupancy the only possible systems which equate marginal costs and benefits. Wage labor will assure efficiency under some, but not all, situations. Taxes on increased production and government payments to farmers to take land out of production can also reduce food production. So can a pattern of land and resource ownership that leaves many people with low incomes while a few owners receive most of the returns. This last arrangement can lead to underuse of agricultural land, compared to nutritional needs, even if markets transmit incentives to producers effectively because the prices of luxuries are bid up compared to the prices of food. Patterns of ownership and other institutions thus can decrease the availability of food to a society by leading to underproduction, just as in the case of the commons they may reduce food availability by causing temporary overuse of resources.

REINVESTMENT AND GROWTH

The institutions discussed above affect the efficiency with which existing resources are used. But the resources available to food production may also be expanded by reinvestment. Attainment of higher levels of production will certainly require investment in irrigation and drainage of new lands, in fertilizer factories and farm machinery, and in supporting and marketing facilities for agriculture. Reinvestment by a farm may be affected by the individual incentives that the producer faces. It may be affected even more, however, by institutions that operate at the level of the national economic system as a whole.

The effect of overall economic systems on growth is shown most strikingly in the contrasts between the economies of Japan and Java since these two large islands off the coasts of Asia were first contacted by Europeans. Both cases can only be interpreted in the light of the ecological possibilities of their local environments: their soils, climates, water supplies, and possibilities for different species to grow. Each case involves analysis of population growth patterns. But the basic institutions adopted by or imposed on the two societies seem to account for the eventual success of Japanese development, and the failure of the economy of Java.[10]

The Underdeveloping of Java

The islands of Indonesia were originally covered with tropical forest. Before the Dutch conquest in the seventeenth century, a few million people, at

[10] Clifford Geertz, *Agricultural Involution* (Berkeley: University of California Press, 1963), *passim*.

most, lived there. Some lived in scattered groups, practicing slash and burn agriculture; others lived in small kingdoms where intensive agriculture was possible. These were sections of Java where fresh mineral nutrients were constantly provided for the soil by volcanic activity. Streams washed minerals from the volcanic mountains to the lowlands, where they were dammed up, and diverted to flood rice fields. In this system of agriculture, called *sawah* in Java, water provided nutrients to the crop and the tropical sunlight provided energy. Once irrigation systems and terraces had been built, a relatively high standard of living was possible. The sawah cultivators could derive a surplus above subsistence to support their courts and sultans in a way that the slash and burn cultivation could not.

Dutch colonization was a commercial venture; the government itself was run by the Netherlands West India Company. Even after control reverted to the Dutch crown, governors were given export revenue targets. On some of the islands, coffee, tobacco, spices, and eventually rubber were exported. These crops could be grown on slash and burn plots, without disrupting forest ecology or local food supplies. But sugar turned out to be the most profitable crop Java could produce. Cane could be grown on the irrigated terraces also used for sawah rice. The peasant villages that lived off the rice were also a handy source of labor for the sugar harvest, which requires large gangs of cutters. The Dutch saw this would allow high profits if they could organize production without having to pay high wages for the labor or rents for the land. At first, the Dutch tried requiring local sultans to give them sugar as tribute. Later, taxes in cash were levied on villages, forcing them to grow sugar for sale. In 1830, Governor Van Den Bosch introduced a new institution, which was to be profitable for the Netherlands, and disastrous for Java.

Under the "culture system," villages were freed from taxes in return for lending one-fifth of their land to the government for sugar cultivation. The portion of the sawah land loaned would be changed each year, to permit crop rotation between flooded rice cultivation, and drainage for sugar. The mountain streams would thus provide the nutrients for both crops. People without sawah land to share with the government were required to provide sixty-six days of work each year. This gave the government a labor force to harvest cane, and to build new irrigation systems and terraces.

The culture system allowed a rapid expansion of both sugar and rice production. At the outset, the Javanese had been producing more than enough rice to subsist. They had been able to support their sultans and pay the first Dutch tributes and taxes without using all of their possible working time. The culture system made them work harder; it transferred the excess capacity of existing fields to sugar growing. Leisure time was given up to new construction. The same process continued when the Dutch replaced the culture system with corporate plantations. After 1870, the government got out of the sugar producing business itself, but it forced villages to rent more than one-third of their sawah lands to Dutch companies and to provide labor to them at low wages to harvest cane and build new terraces.

53

Early in the twentieth century, Java ran out of new land for terracing. Population had grown rapidly, as a result of the initial increase in rice production. Then, the Dutch instituted an "ethical system," designed to improve living conditions in their colony. They increased wages and improved their public health services in Java. This, of course, helped ensure a continued high rate of population growth. Increasing population, combined with the end of enforced low wages, made the demand for rice press on land availability. Some plantations ceased sugar cultivation, and the land returned to rice growing. Others continued to hire labor, but most labor had to be used to cultivate rice. As population increased, it was possible to feed the population only by increasing per-acre rice production.

The possibility of this intensification was the great strength of sawah agriculture. Rice cultivation per acre could be increased by increasing the amount of nutrients in the paddy fields through more frequent flooding and draining; through an intensification of weeding to ensure that the increased nutrients were used by rice; and through increased transplanting and trimming required in the process. However, the labor requirements for this cultivation were severe. After a time, virtually all of the labor time of a growing population had to be devoted to the rice fields, to ensure sustenance for all. Each additional hand only added enough new product to feed the corresponding new mouth.

By the time Indonesia achieved independence, virtually all the sugar plantations in Java had been abandoned. The sawah lands had been returned to rice cultivation. The cultivated area was far greater than it had been in 1830, and population had grown almost tenfold. A considerable investment in labor had been made, and major engineering works built. But when it was all over, there was less margin for new investment in Java than on the eve of Van Den Bosch's governorship. The people could not feed themselves with only part of their potential effort. They could no longer secure their sustenance, afford taxes to the new government that had replaced the sultans and the Dutch, and still have much time left over for leisure or for work on new investments. For the time, new population could still be accommodated by further intensification of sawah cultivation, but even the limits of this could be perceived. Increased population would at some point threaten to overrun resources.

The Developing of Japan

The beginnings of the story of Japan's modernization are not too different from the first chapters of the underdeveloping of Java. In the sixteenth century, population density may have even been somewhat greater than that of Indonesia, and rice yields lower. Japan had some irrigated cultivation of rice, but fewer natural advantages of tropical climate and rich streams. However, in the seventeenth century, as Indonesia fell under Dutch rule, Japan's contacts with the West were terminated soon after their inception. A strong central government, the Tokugawa Shogunate, closed Japan's borders to foreigners, and imposed a

54

hierarchical feudal organization in agriculture. The peasants were guaranteed peace, after a long period of disorder, in return for taxes to support the dynasty and its warrior retainers. During nearly three centuries of Tokugawa rule, agricultural productivity rose slowly, through the introduction of commercial fertilizers, new threshing devices, and other improvements. By the middle of the nineteenth century, rice yields were similar to those in Java at the time: some sixty or seventy bushels per hectare.

As in Java, rice cultivation at this level did not require all of the potential labor of the Japanese. There was a potential surplus of labor available for investment activities. Up to 1868, this surplus was mostly devoted to maintaining the aristocracy. In that year, however, impelled in part by fear that Japan's sovereignty would be lost to foreign nations, the Meiji Restoration seized power. The new regime not only prevented foreign domination, it also set out to increase Japanese economic productivity. Feudal dues that had consisted of a share of the crop were replaced by a fixed land tax levied on the potential yield of fields. This tax allowed landowners to reap all of the benefits of any productivity increases beyond the presumed initial capacity of their farms. It is generally acknowledged to have contributed greatly to farmers' incentives. At the same time, the government introduced a system of agricultural education, comparable only to the United States's extension service in its scope. This, too, contributed greatly to productivity. Rising productivity allowed the increase in Japanese population to be directed out of agriculture into industry. The number of farm workers remained relatively constant for half a century following the Meiji Restoration. What is more, both government taxes and part of landowners' profits were directed toward industrial investment, which eventually began to return to agriculture farm equipment and fertilizer which could again improve yields. Continued reinvestment allowed further increases in productivity, per man and per acre. Additionally, by the 1960s, industrialization and urban growth had led to a decline in the birth rate and a slower rate of population growth. Japan, unlike Indonesia, had become a developed country. If it faced ecological problems, they were those of pollution, not starvation.

SUMMARY

The rules of the game in economy, and the distribution of power in a society, as well as simple natural and technological factors, may affect the balance between demography and food supply. For Malthus and Ricardo, vice and inequality were the only reliable mechanisms, short of famine, war, and pestilence, to keep population in line with resources. Chapter 2 presented arguments suggesting that equality and economic development might be more effective factors to reduce population growth. Similar considerations affect the other side of the equation: food supply. Some argue that inequality is necessary for growth because large farms are more efficient and progressive than small farms.

55

Large farms do reduce the cost of introducing new technology. However, equal division of land may prevent ecological problems of genetic uniformity of crops, dependence on pesticides, and overurbanization.

Some problems must be faced in designing an agricultural system. Farmers require incentives to produce a surplus of crops for towns and industry. Some taxes or sharecropping systems, as well as deliberate crop limitation policies by government, reduce the incentives to produce. On the other hand, availability of unpriced common resources may lead to attempted overuse. Overgrazing of pastures or other resource depletion may occur, reducing total production. A variety of institutions, from cooperatives or community forms of tenure to individual ownership, may be used to improve incentives. The existence of an agricultural surplus alone does not ensure development. It may be diverted to the use of a colonial power as in Java, or it may be wasted. However, if as in Japan reinvestment leads to economic development, then food supply becomes a less-pressing problem. For most developed countries, other environmental problems become more crucial. They are discussed in the subsequent chapters.

Selected Readings

Several general accounts of agricultural underdevelopment and the Green Revolution are available, with different perspectives. See T. W. Schultz, *Transforming Traditional Agriculture* (New Haven: Yale University Press, 1964); Max F. Millikan and David Hapgood, *No Easy Harvest* (Boston: Little, Brown & Co., 1967); Lester R. Brown, *Seeds of Change* (New York: Praeger, 1970); and Ernest Feder, *The Rape of the Peasantry* (New York: Doubleday, 1971). More general works on economic development include Richard Gill, *Economic Development: Past and Present*, in this series, and Paul A. Baran, *The Political Economy of Growth* (New York: Monthly Review Press, 1957).

In addition to Clifford Geertz, *Agricultural Involution* (Berkeley: University of California Press, 1963), the role of economic, legal, and social institutions in shaping agricultural adaptation to the environment in different areas is explored in Elizabeth Whitcombe, *Agrarian Change in Northern India* (Berkeley: University of California Press, 1971); Michael Even-Ari, *The Negev* (Cambridge, Mass.: Harvard University Press, 1971); William Hinton, *Fanshen* (New York: Monthly Review Press, 1966); Harry M. Caudill, *Night Comes to the Cumberlands* (Boston: Little, Brown & Co., 1963); and the essays in Andrew Vayda, ed., *Environment and Cultural Behavior* (Garden City: Doubleday, 1969).

Growth,

Pollution, and Social Cost

CHAPTER FOUR

Inadequate food supply is not the only possible imbalance in the flow of materials and energy between human society and its environment. When agriculture advances enough that some workers can turn from farming to other tasks, this division of labor can produce economic growth. Then new problems may occur: depletion of raw materials needed for the new activities, environmental pollution from energy use on a massive scale, interruption of nutrient cycles by the concentration of population in cities, and overtaxing of the environment's capacity to absorb and recycle waste products. This chapter discusses the origins and form of these interrelated problems. Proposals for amelioration of these problems are considered in later chapters.

This chapter reviews how economic development in the West led to pressure on the environment, and raises the issue of whether complete cessation of economic development, *zero GNP growth*, is a necessary condition for ecological balance. Some possibilities for ecologically sound growth are suggested, but ways are shown in which economic institutions create incentives for individuals or groups to destroy the environment. This discussion develops the concepts of *social costs* and *external diseconomies* as failures in economic systems.

THE ORIGINS OF IMBALANCE

The Division of Labor

Pollution and conservation problems, as we know them, are a result of economic growth. This does not mean that all economic growth necessarily disrupts material and energy cycles, but, without an increase in the tools and technologies used by the human economy, the problems could not have occurred. Only when food for a population could be produced by less than the full-time labor of the whole society, could large amounts of work be expended on mining and manufacturing. Only then, could new metals and energy sources be added as inputs into the economy, or modern cities and worldwide systems of bulk transportation be developed. The division of labor was necessary before so many materials could be brought together, or so much energy used—sometimes for human welfare, but sometimes in such places, times, and quantities as to endanger life.

An agricultural surplus does not necessarily induce growth. With increasing productivity, people may increase their leisure or their numbers without leaving the land or seeking out new materials and energy sources. But, from the earliest times, civilizations devised ways to draw population and materials to royal courts, garrisons, and ceremonial or trade centers, and to organize labor for new activities. The industrial revolution and the rise of capitalism, however, redirected labor from farming to new activities on an unprecedented scale. Workers were drawn into new activities in many ways. Some came voluntarily, to seek their fortunes, or to earn wages to buy new industrial consumer goods. Particularly in the early stages of industrialization, force was also used. Slaves were brought from Africa to the mines and plantations of the Americas. Convicts were "transported," and sailors shanghaied into service. Families thrown off the land, by enclosures in England and the later "tearing down" of farms in Germany, had to seek employment at a subsistence wage in cities. The competition of new products and technologies also left many farmers and artisans bankrupt, forcing them to seek industrial employment. One way or another, populations were redistributed: from farms and small towns, to industrial and mercantile centers, to mining camps, and to plantations so specialized in one crop they had to import food.[1]

This new division of labor created possibilities for advances in human standards of living. People could use new products; life expectancies increased and some major diseases were conquered. Even Marx, in his critiques of capitalism, argued it fulfilled an important historical mission by developing technological potential. Of course, the gains were not equally distributed. The workers torn from the land had no choice but to accept work for subsistence pay, at least until they organized to demand better wages, hours, and working conditions, and until industrialization had reached the point at which the employers could grant some of these demands and still keep profits to reinvest. Nor were the gains won without a cost to the environment. Under existing institutions, industrialization, urbanization, and the use of new materials created problems of material supply, congestion, and waste disposal.

[1] Stephen Hymer, "The Multinational Corporation and the Law of Uneven Development," in *Economic and World Order*, J. Bhagwati, ed. (New York: Macmillan, 1972).

Waste disposal is a necessary activity of all societies, even those with purely agricultural economies. When land is plowed, there is some runoff of organic materials. The simplest cooking fire releases smoke and carbon dioxide into the atmosphere. Human life, like any life, leaves organic wastes. But the manner in which waste is disposed can vary. Chinese peasants, too poor in resources to afford even small losses of nutrients from their ecosystems, were careful to build outhouses that allowed a return of human excrement to the fields. Where population pressure was great enough, the labor used to spread night soil bore enough return in crops to justify the effort. Other preindustrial societies, practicing slash-and-burn agriculture with lower population densities, could allow the wind to carry off elements in the form of ash. European explorers encountering these societies at burning season, reported that clouds of smoke affected the climate, trapping moisture and bringing rain. These clouds that hung over the present sites of Los Angeles and Mexico City now appear to have been precursors of smog. But they were only a brief annual episode, part of the process of feeding a population in the most effective way possible. As the case of the Tsembaga shows, when population pressure is not too great, even slash-and-burn agriculture can be stable. The winds that blow nutrients from one field drop them on other fields or forests.

The simplest societies, therefore, faced either the cost in labor of recycling, or the annoyance of smoke and the risk of soil deterioration, from burning. Both the Tsembaga and the Chinese systems were, in a sense, methods of recycling materials. At times, recycling is simple if residence and agriculture are closely linked. At other times, the natural waste-dispersal properties of wind and water will do the job slowly but without human effort. Ash returns to the soil. Carbon dioxide from combustion is dispersed by the atmosphere. Eventually, some of it is used in photosynthesis. Using the energy of sunlight, plants produce sugars, and release oxygen back into the atmosphere. Similarly, the oceans absorb carbon dioxide. Some of the dissolved carbon dioxide is then used for photosynthesis by marine plankton.

Flowing water can degrade biological waste. When there is dissolved oxygen in water, oxygen-using bacteria decompose organic matter. Only if all of the oxygen is used up by these bacteria, will the remaining organic matter be decomposed by anaerobic bacteria. Then, a stench will be created and other aquatic life will fail for want of oxygen. Similarly, the soil, and the bacteria and fungi it harbors can decompose some organic wastes without disrupting life, and disperse concentrations of chemical compounds. Noise, too, creates no problems when each loud sound dies away before many others clash with it.

Use of these natural environmental properties for waste removal and treatment is not dangerous pollution. It is, rather, an economical (from man's view-

60

point) and nondisruptive method of passing materials on from human uses to other points in the flow of materials between populations and environments in nature. It is a link between the input-output flows of the human economy, and those of natural ecosystems. Economists are skeptical of those who claim that people should never dump wastes into the environment: sometimes it is cheaper, and not disruptive of any other species, to let nature take its course with discharged wastes. Until recently, deliberate waste collection was employed only rarely, when nutrient scarcity required waste materials to be used more quickly by man than if they were allowed to disperse, and in very rare cases in which the wastes were themselves a nuisance.

Pollution and Congestion

Nonrecycled wastes of pollution first became a problem in ancient cities. The Romans complained of the dumping of chamber pots, the noise of chariots, and other problems of congestion.[2] By the nineteenth century, sanitation was a serious problem for many European cities. On some days, the British Parliament did not meet because of the smell of sewage in the Thames. Urban crowding created other problems as well. Teeming areas with bad sanitation were susceptible to epidemics. Food shortages also became a problem. A city generally is a concentrated population removed from its sources of food. Provisioning urban areas requires a more intensive utilization of nearby soil than does a purely rural population. The pressure on land to feed the cities, discussed earlier, may have contributed to the failure of ancient civilizations. Removal of so many nutrients from the country to the city created problems for the return of nutrients to the soil. As the nineteenth century biologist, Justus Liebig, pointed out, the wastes of cities were dumped in waterways, like the Thames, and not returned to the land.[3] These problems of pollution and provisioning became more important with the growth of cities in the twentieth century, but they are not entirely new.

In addition to concentrating human population and human wastes in cities, nineteenth and twentieth century industrial growth brought new materials and energy sources into use. Some of the materials used in industry were poisonous to life, or could become so in certain concentrations or compounds. Others, particularly some chemicals and plastics developed in the twentieth century, are not degradable by the environment. Energy use was expanded to the point at which the heat and smoke, and even the carbon dioxide produced, could become problems. Treating and combining these unprecedented quantities of materials required considerable caution on the part of human society, if its economy was not to overtax the waste absorption capacities of the natural environment,

[2] Juvenal, *Satires.*
[3] Justus Liebig, *Die Chemie,* cited in Frederick Engels, *The Housing Question* (1872) (New York: International Publishers, n.d.).

and if it were not to destroy its own sources of supply of at least some materials. The institutions under which growth occurred, however, were not generally conducive to this caution.

Environmental problems first became a public policy issue in England in the 1860s. In the previous generation, the British had attempted to adopt the institutions of a free market. Businesses could do as they wished, restrained only by competition. Free trade and competition were conducive to rapid growth in the economy, but after a time, the British government began to reimpose restraints. To the conservatives of the time, these acts seemed evidence of a conspiracy against the market. However, Karl Polanyi has argued that the first interferences were generally to solve environmental problems created by the market. The first acts provided for "analysts of food and drink," inspectors of gasworks, enforced vaccination, inspectors for the "wholesomeness or unwholesomeness of food," regulation of rural drainage and water supply, regulation of transportation, some limits to employment of child labor, and minimal safety regulations for mines and chimney sweepers. According to Polanyi, English society was reacting against market institutions, which were threatening to disrupt its very environmental and social fabric.[4] Of course, in the case of some factory reforms, it was not society as a whole but specifically the pressure of labor organizations that forced change. But even after those changes, the institutions of the economy still allowed considerable environmental disruption.

In the twentieth century, and particularly since the outbreak of World War II, uses of energy and materials have increased at a rapid rate. Table 4–1 shows the growth of energy use in the more industrialized countries. Consumption of metals has shown a similar increase. The growth of energy and materials use alone would create serious problems to be resolved in the treatment or disposal of residuals, as well as in the conservation of energy supplies. But the problem has been made worse by the invention and widespread use of many new substitutes which are not degraded by natural forces. Barry Commoner has argued that "the chief reason for the environmental crisis that has engulfed the United States in recent years is the sweeping transformation of productive technology since World War II . . . productive technologies with intense impacts on the environment have displaced less destructive ones."[5] Commoner cites the use of artificial fertilizers in place of organic fertilizers, the use of synthetics and plastics in place of materials occurring in natural form, replacement of soap by detergents, and other examples of "technological displacement." Table 4–2 shows different forms of pollution. Some are local in their impact, and some global. Some appear to present major threats to life, others only nuisances. Along with these, the depletion of some raw materials also threatened to disrupt the economy. A century after environmental protection became a matter for public policies in England, it finally became a crisis issue perceived by public opinion in the United States and other countries.

[4] Karl Polanyi, *The Great Transformation* (Boston: Beacon Press, 1957).
[5] Barry Commoner, *The Closing Circle* (New York: Alfred A. Knopf, 1971), p. 177.

Table 4–1   ENERGY USE AND INCOME, PER CAPITA

Country	Energy Consumption Per Capita (Coal Equivalent Metric Tons) 1966	Per Capita Gross Domestic Product (U.S. Dollars) 1965
United States	9619	3536
Canada	7925	2505
Czechoslovakia	5594	1300
East Germany	5498	1270
United Kingdom	5088	1790
Sweden	5037	2487
Australia	4664	1593
Belgium	4601	1761
Denmark	4436	2109
West Germany	4256	1977
Norway	3932	1532
Soviet Union	3791	1150
Netherlands	3570	1532
Poland	3568	820
France	2976	1922
Hungary	2834	940
Switzerland	2732	2301
Austria	2679	1287
South Africa	2668	590
Romania	2100	620
Italy	1962	1100
Japan	1945	870
Israel	1734	1407
Argentina	1368	670
Yugoslavia	1203	370
Spain	1122	600
Chile	1087	573
Greece	847	673
Portugal	506	400
China	448	100
Brazil	387	273
India	174	102
Indonesia	100	70

Sources: *United Nations Statistical Yearbook*, 1970; E. E. Hagen and O. Hawrylyshyn, "Analysis of World Income and Growth," *Economic Development and Cultural Change*, Vol. 18, No. 1, October 1969, Part II.

Table 4–2 FORMS OF POLLUTION

Type of Pollutant	Trends in Extent	Natural Recycling
VISIBLE OBJECTS AND SMOKE: discarded objects (cans, waste paper, etc.); waste from industry (slag heaps, mine tailings); ash and particles in air; rubble from buildings	Much not new; some forms decreasing (railroad smoke); overall weight increases with growth; some new materials less easy to recycle.	Smoke precipitates; objects worn down by wind or water, but speeds vary. Some modern synthetics particularly durable. Raw materials may be so dispersed that reuse in same form never possible (e.g.: nutrients or metals dissolved in ocean).
ORGANIC WASTES AND FERTILIZERS: human and animal wastes; consumed foods; other organic waste; materials (nitrates, phosphates) which lead to rapid growth of algae.	Organic wastes generally increase with population, consumption, and industrial material use; large cities increase recycling problems; phosphate and nitrate use has increased rapidly.	In low concentrations, decay occurs in water or moist soil. Burning, or decay, release nutrient elements which may return to soil, or to lakes and oceans. In high concentrations, natural decomposition by aerobic bacteria breaks down.
LOCAL AIR POLLUTION: smoke; carbon monoxide from incomplete combustion; nitrogen oxides from hot fires; sulphur oxides; photochemical smog (hydrocarbons reacting chemically in the air).	Quantity of emissions (other than smoke) rose with recent energy and auto use; concentration of population in cities increased concentration of pollutants in air.	Pollutants are dispersed by wind and eventually precipitated out of air or absorbed in water. Local concentrations may rise beyond dispersal level at times; persistence and photochemical reactions greatest, locally, in temperature inversions.
WORLDWIDE ATMOSPHERIC POLLUTION: Carbon dioxide; dust clouds. (Not dangerous at local level, but increases in worldwide level may affect climate).	Measured CO_2 is rising at more than 0.2% per year. Dust clouds in upper atmosphere also are increasing.	Natural cycles in CO_2 and dust levels existed before industry (e.g. due to volcanic action); both dust and CO_2 normally dissolve in ocean and CO_2 used in plant photosynthesis.
PERSISTENT TOXIC MATERIALS: Chlorinated hydrocarbons (DDT); heavy metals (lead, mercury, cadmium) in air and water and absorbed by organisms.	Use of chlorinated hydrocarbon insecticides is new; use of heavy metals increased in industrialization. Concentrations of these metals in ocean and in bodies of sea life may have increased.	DDT degraded and heavy metals absorbed in inert compounds only slowly. Materials absorbed by algae, or swallowed, are retained by organism and concentrated further in bodies of predators which eat many times own weight in organisms.
HEAT, NOISE, RADIOACTIVITY: These are forms of energy, not materials. Sonic booms, high decibel sounds, heat from power plants, atomic contamination and fallout.	Atomic energy use, and technologies which can create heat and noise problems, are recent developments.	Radiation can be carried by long-lived radioactive isotopes, such as strontium 90, which act as persistent pollutants. Otherwise, energy contaminants die down or disperse with time and distance.
CONGESTION: High density of occupation, or population, in an area not only increases other forms of pollution, but acts directly like forms of pollution, from an economic viewpoint.	Cities, and concentrations of economic activity, have increased over time.	No natural retarding process in humans. In some species, high densities appear to retard reproduction.

Table 4–2   FORMS OF POLLUTION (cont.)

Damage Done	Treatment
Fire and health hazards from organic garbage; smoke, a local problem "on wrong side of the tracks;" rubble increases costs of reusing land; blocking of waterways by solids, and disruption of wetland ecosystems; many forms of aesthetic damage (automobile graveyards, litter, etc.).	Removal of solid waste from large towns is costly; land used for dumps may be removed from other use (although some landfill can enhance land for other uses); manual labor often the main factor in removal: voluntary antilitter drives popular because results easy and visible.
Exhaustion of oxygen in water if large quantities of organic waste (or of algae fertilized by inorganic materials) raise demand for oxygen in decomposition. Other life unable to survive, and septic decay by anaerobic bacteria causes stench and health hazards. If wastes not decomposed and separated from habitation and from food and water supplies, disease carriers may be harbored.	In areas of low population concentration, simple latrines and sewers to separate undecomposed waste from water or food supply. In urban areas, waste removal is expensive. Sewage treatment, prior to return to waterways, reduces load on oxygen supply. Spreading of sewage over land, or treatment to extract natural fertilizer, prevents loss of nutrients from land to oceans, but is costly. No feasible treatment yet for nitrate or phosphate overload.
Local weather modification; danger to health. In high concentrations, smog, carbon monoxide, nitrogen oxides, and sulphur oxides all linked statistically to levels of lung diseases and other diseases. Several disasters, involving many deaths, have occurred from local temporary concentrations during temperature inversions. Sulphur oxides also a source of damage to buildings and other property.	Possibilities for cleaner burning to reduce carbon monoxide, smoke, and hydrocarbon levels exist, but may increase nitrogen oxide levels. Cleaner fuels or "scrubbing" of smoke may reduce particulate and sulphur dioxide levels. Wastes previously disposed of by burning may be removed by other means. Relocation of some industrial activities may reduce concentrations of pollutants in particular locations.
Increasing CO_2 concentrations trap heat in the atmosphere, creating a warming trend. Dust in atmosphere reflects solar radiation into space, creating a cooling trend. At present, the two trends appear to offset each other, but they may not do so indefinitely.	Research on worldwide atmospheric pollution, and on its effects on climate, is still at an early stage. Shifting to alternate energy sources besides fuel combustion would be required to reduce CO_2 emissions.
Ingested by animals, DDT remains in food chains. In birds, it inhibits the use of calcium in egg shells, and inhibits reproduction. Effects on other animals are less clear. Heavy metals attack the central nervous system. Concentrations by some of these pollutants are believed by some scientists to be at a dangerous level on a worldwide scale.	Local lead contamination in cities may require removal of lead additives from gasoline used in automobiles. Heavy metal pollution can be cut by more careful waste recapture in industry, and removal of lead paint in slum dwellings. New insecticides, biological control of pests, and restrictions on DDT use appear to be the only means of limiting chlorinated hydrocarbon levels.
Somatic and genetic damage from radiation; damage to equipment and psychological damage from noise; disruption of natural ecosystems by changes in temperature.	Shielding of radiation and disposal of radioactive materials require development of new and expensive technologies, still not entirely safe. Heat dispersal equipment (e.g. evaporation towers), and noise abatement equipment can be developed.
Effect of crowding on human psychology uncertain. Experiments on animals suggest damage. Crowding of same species increases probabilities of epidemic disease. Transportation, recreation, and other activities can be impaired by simple fact of individuals getting in each others' way.	If crowding were a phenomenon affecting the entire globe, only population reduction or control would be possible. Since crowding is localized, technologies for transport or communication, or new economic or political institutions might reduce need for crowding.

IS ZERO GROWTH NECESSARY?

The historical association between economic growth and environmental problems has led some commentators to argue that society is faced with an inescapable choice. Either it can give up growth and reduce material consumption levels, or it can destroy the environment and imperil human survival. Just as Malthus argued that population growth induced by prosperity would outrun food supply and lead to misery, several writers now argue that economic growth itself will cause misery. Others, however, argue that some forms of growth and increased living standards may be compatible with ecological preservation.

The "Zero GNP Growth" Argument

Many people argue that economic growth must necessarily increase pollution. Edwin L. Dale, Jr., of the *New York Times*, has written,

> There are, alas, a few 'iron laws' that cannot be escaped in the effort to reduce the pollution of our air and water, in disposing of solid waste and the like . . . The hard fact is: growth of production is the basic cause of pollution growth.[6]

The only way to limit pollution significantly, in this view, is to reduce production. Dale argues, however, that this would cause massive unemployment. Because the U.S. labor force increases one percent a year, and potential per worker productivity increases by as much as three percent, full-time work for all requires the economy to continue to grow at 4 percent a year or double production every eighteen years. "The law of economic growth, then, tells us a simple truth: 'we' cannot choose to reduce production simply because we have found it to be the cause of a fouled environment." Dale does not call efforts against pollution completely useless. He argues for incentives to encourage production in the least-polluting manner possible, and for some government spending for pollution abatement. Reduction in population growth could produce long-run relief, and technology might be improved to reduce pollution. "But, in the end, we cannot be sure that the job will be done."

A more dismal prospect, yet, is derived when rigid links between pollution and both population and production are assumed. Computer simulations on those assumptions have been made by Jay W. Forrester and by the "Club of Rome," a group of businessman and management experts.[7] Their models seek

[6] Edwin L. Dale, Jr., "The Economics of Pollution," *New York Times Magazine*, April 19, 1970, p. 27.

[7] Jay W. Forrester, *World Dynamics* (Cambridge, Mass.: Wright-Allen Press, 1971); The Club of Rome, *The Limits to Growth* (New York: Universe Books, 1972).

to test the effects that continued population and industrial growth will have on "the predicament of mankind." The models assume that the mineral resource capacity, food producing capacity of the earth, and waste dispersal capacity of the environment have fixed limits. As population and industrial capacity grow, they are assumed to increase demand for the three fixed capacities. Each time the computer is used to predict the future, it must base its predictions on a set of equations relating the demands for these three capacities to industrial growth or population growth rates. In turn, population and production are assumed to grow at an exponential rate, with relatively short "doubling times," unless one of the three capacities is very near exhaustion. If, however, food supply capacity drops to subsistence, minerals are exhausted, or waste disposal capacity overtaxed by pollution, then the equations involve an assumption of rapid population or industrial decline. The relationships assumed ensure that a computer prediction of the future will show rapid growth for a time, followed by a rapid decline in population or income, once a capacity limit is hit. One such prediction is depicted in Fig. 4–1.

The result is an alarming prediction, to be sure. Famine, massive deaths

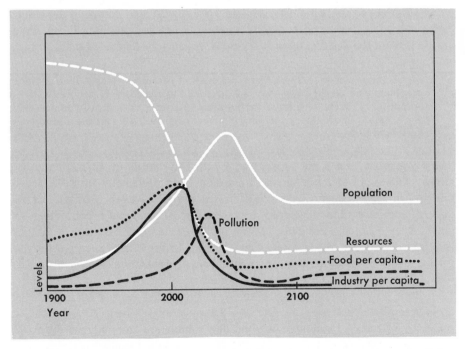

FIG. 4–1 Computer projection assuming rigid links between population, output, and pollution. (Source: Donella and Dennis Meadows *et. al.*, for The Club of Rome, *The Limits to Growth* (New York: Universe Books, 1972). This is one of a series of computer-generated scenarios. Each is based on arbitrary assumption about relations between the five variables shown, to demonstrate how they might relate to each other.)

from pollution, or industrial collapse seem inevitable unless growth is halted soon. Wide publicity given to the computers' elegant graphs is used to stimulate a sense of urgency, or just plain fear. Essentially, however, the picture is not new, even if Forrester argues that "complex systems are counterintuitive," and only the computer can see where mankind is going. The assumptions are essentially those of Malthus, except that industry is assumed to act like population, and pollution, or mineral depletion, to act like famine. The essential ideas are the same, however. Like Malthus, Forrester and the Club of Rome leave out possibilities. A negative effect of income growth on population, a shift in production away from polluting products, and increased recycling all could change the relations that underlie the model. Nor is convincing evidence presented for the assumption that exhaustion of one of the three capacities will lead to a sudden collapse of civilization, rather than a slow development of symptoms of trouble, which can signal humanity to act in time. The computer can draw pictures of many possible futures, but it cannot determine which ones are correct. The computer always bases its conclusions on the assumptions of its programmers and, as computer users say, the result may be "garbage in, garbage out."

Whether based on the Rome model, or on more direct perceptions that industry is causing pollution, some writers have begun calling for *zero GNP growth* as well as *zero population growth*. They suggest that people in the United States and other developed countries must reduce their per capita living standards to prevent the destruction of mankind. One analysis concluded that

> considerations of the environment and natural resources require that optimum production be set at a low, constant level . . . a considerably reduced GNP is feasible . . . What will have to be done without is the grossly materialistic consumption and military spending both we and the U.S. economy have come to depend upon.[8]

These arguments, when put forward at "Earth Day" teach-ins in 1970 and at a United Nations Conference on the Environment at Stockholm in 1972, led to criticism of the environmentalists' position. Representatives of poor nations and poor minorities within developed countries denied they were consuming too much. They claimed an attempt to stop growth would deprive them of the possibilities of a decent standard of living, in order to provide cleaner playgrounds for the rich. Many denied that an environmental problem existed at all; others, like Dale, simply argued for living with pollution.

Both proponents and opponents of growth often neglect to ask whether ecological destruction and poverty are the only alternatives. Are the choices really so extreme? Economic growth, like population growth, can obviously exceed the capacities of the environment at some point. Eventually, stable popu-

[8] John Hardesty, Norris C. Clement, and Clinton E. Jencks, "The Political Economy of Environmental Destruction," in W. A. Johnson and J. Hardesty, *Economic Growth vs. the Environment* (Belmont, Cal.: Wadsworth, 1971), p. 105.

lation and output will be necessary for survival. But is the world already at the point where further growth is impossible? An argument can be presented that an immediate attempt to prevent material standards of living from rising is not necessary. The zero GNP growth argument may ignore possibilities for different forms of growth which would be less destructive of the environment. It also assumes too close a link between the Gross National Product, as it is measured today, and living standards. Perhaps not all growth need necessarily lead to disaster.

Possibilities of Substitution

The first weakness in the link between GNP and pollution, is that not all activities entering into GNP create the same amount of pollution. Ten dollars spent on driving for pleasure will involve more combustion than ten dollars spent on an evening at the theater, unless the theater has exceptionally high heating bills. A million dollars spent on operation of a jet bomber will cause more pollution than a similar sum spent on parks—unless the latter require large amounts of automobile transport. A billion dollars spent on investments in industry will have different effects from a billion dollars spent on sewage treatment plants.

Some of the variation in pollution between different sectors of GNP can be traced with the aid of the input-output tables for the United States economy. As explained in Chapter 1, these tables show the value of products purchased by each industry from each other industry. From these tables, others are derived which show the number of dollars' worth of goods which are required, directly or indirectly, from every other industry, for the production of a given value of any one good. Thus, it is possible to compute the number of dollars' worth of raw petroleum entering into the production of a thousand dollars' worth of shoes, ships, or sealing wax. Because petroleum combustion is one major source of air pollution, these figures give some idea of the atmospheric destructiveness of different industries. Other tables could also be developed that show the direct output of different wastes in the production of different goods. These *material balance* tables would be more accurate than present input-output tables, because input-output tables used here include not only petroleum used for fuel, but also the petroleum used as raw materials for plastics, or for fertilizer, and because the cleanliness of combustion varies among industries.

The input-output requirements are computed by looking at averages for the United States economy in a given year. (The figures used here are for 1963). They do not reflect the possibilities that could occur with other technologies. Even using these 1963 relations, there are some systematic differences among different sectors of the economy in their needs for petroleum. Table 4–3 shows the spending on crude petroleum that is created by a thousand dollars spent by consumers; federal, and state, or local, governments; private investors; and foreign consumers of United States exports. The figures assume that additional

Table 4–3 INPUTS OF PETROLEUM (DIRECT OR INDIRECT) IN GOODS
DEMANDED BY FINAL USER SECTORS
(In millions of dollars and percent of total)

Final Demand Sector	Total Purchases	Petroleum Inputs	Petroleum per Billion $ Products
Personal Consumption	375,540 (63.6%)	8782 (71.6%)	23.1
Private Fixed Capital Formation	80,510 (13.6%)	1067 (8.7%)	13.3
Inventory Change	5,329 (0.9%)	184 (1.5%)	34.5
Gross Exports	5,812 (1.0%)	760 (6.2%)	130.8
Federal Government	64,115 (10.9%)	822 (6.7%)	12.8
State and Local Government	59,082 (10.0%)	650 (5.3%)	11.0
Totals	590,389 (100.0%)	12,265 (100.0%)	20.8

Sources: Input-Output Tables for 1963, in U.S. Department of Commerce, *Survey of Current Business*, November 1969.

thousands of dollars spent by each buyer will be spent in the same proportion on different products, as was done in 1963, and that producing industries will increase their inputs of petroleum proportionately with output. The value given does not include the value added to the crude petroleum by the refining industry, nor does it include transport, warehousing, and retailing expenses on the finished products. The figures given refer to the goods as they leave the factory.

As Table 4–3 shows, demand by state and local governments, on the average, is for goods and services that use less petroleum than those demanded by others. Transferring a billion dollars from expenditure by the federal government to expenditure by the states, would reduce petroleum use by 1.8 million dollars; a transfer of a billion dollars from private fixed capital formation to state and local expenditure, would reduce petroleum use by 2.3 million. A transfer from other uses to consumer expenditures, as constituted in 1963, would have increased petroleum use, however.

This might appear, at first glance, to bear out Dale's view that pollution is directly related to consumer well-being. As *Newsweek* magazine wrote in response to the teach-ins,

> The villain of the piece is not some profit-hungry industrialist nor some lax public official who can be replaced. The villains are consumers who demand, or at least let themselves be cajoled into demanding new, more, faster, cheaper, bigger playthings without counting the cost in a dirtier, smaller, sicklier world.[9]

But this is a superficial view. If consumer expenditures are divided by type, as they are in Table 4–4, it is clear that many consumer goods use less petroleum in their production than the goods demanded, on the average, by governments

[9] *Newsweek*, May 4, 1970.

Table 4–4 INPUTS OF PETROLEUM (DIRECT OR INDIRECT) IN CON-
SUMER GOODS AND SERVICES
(in millions of dollars)

Industry	Personal Consumption	Petroleum Inputs	Petroleum per Billion $ Product
Wholesale and retail trade	80,791	790	9.81
Real estate and rental	53,878	440	8.04
Food and kindred products	49,921	673	13.47
Medical, educational nonprofit	29,335	190	6.47
Finance and insurance	16,879	116	6.19
Motor vehicles	15,381	130	8.42
Apparel	13,697	155	8.84
Hotels and personal services	12,074	117	9.75
Public utilities	11,358	1070	94.32
Petroleum refinery products	8,232	4200	507.43
Transport and warehousing	8,946	232	26.05
Imports	6,004	n.a.	n.a.
Communications	5,542	32	5.74
Auto repair and services	6,693	70	10.45
Drugs, cleaning, and toilet preparations	5,428	77	14.23
(All other categories)	51,583	590	11.44
Total	375,540	8782	23.14

Source: Input-Output Tables for 1963, in U.S. Department of Commerce, Survey of Current Business, November 1969.

or investors. Only food and drugs, cleaning, and toilet preparations use slightly more. The big difference comes in direct consumer expenditure on "Petroleum Refinery Products" (of which gasoline for automobiles is the most important), "Public Utilities" (electric, gas, water, and sanitary services), and "Transport and Warehousing" (which involve carrying of goods from factory to consumer). The high level of consumer petroleum use, therefore, seems to be a result of the pattern of transport, which will be discussed in Chapter 6.

The input-output table thus shows that different amounts of petroleum might be used if similar levels of total output were divided differently among consumers, investors, or government purchasers, or among different kinds of consumer goods. Figures for metal use, pulp and paper use, and the employment of various other materials involving pollution in their production or consumption could be computed on similar principles, from the input-output table. They, too, would show some variation among kinds of demand. The differences shown might not be great. The input-output table only shows what could be done using the average technologies in use in 1963. But it does raise a possibility that different levels of pollution might be possible for the same total GNP.

A second weakness, in linking GNP and pollution, is that this ignores possibilities for reducing pollution through recycling. Waste products may be absorbed by the atmosphere, water, or other species, or they may be conserved in dumps or other storage facilities. In these cases, they are often disruptive to ecosystems or to human sensibilities. But they may also be reused as inputs into new productive processes. Scrap metals and waste paper have often been reprocessed for use. In some cities, sewage is beginning to be processed for production of fertilizers. Sulphur scrubbed from the smoke of coal-burning electric plants could be returned to the market. These activities have a high cost, so that businesses have generally not undertaken them except in periods of resources scarcities such as wars. Because the total resources of the earth are limited, however, writers on ecology have pointed out that maintaining resource supplies indefinitely would require the use of what are now considered wastes.

Possibilities for recycling can be traced, using an extension of input-output frameworks.[10] In the expanded *materials balance approach*, materials are not treated as dropping out of the economy when they are "used up" by producers or consumers, as occurs in an ordinary input-output table. Rather, the amount of different wastes and residuals, and the energy expanded, are listed as additional outputs. So, for example, a producer of steel is listed as producing not only steel, but also chemical wastes, slag, and waste heat energy. The inputs of different resources, and the outputs of different goods, wastes, and energy must be related by physical and chemical laws. In this accounting framework, it can be shown that different wastes can be substituted for each other (as when a factory elects whether to burn its wastes, flush them into sewers, dump them as solids, or reprocess them), and how the end products of economic activity relate to the original raw materials. Clearly, if the same materials are processed and reprocessed several times, rather than being wasted at the end of each process, the net amount of economic activity can increase without using up more of the material. This would be another way in which increased GNP might be compatible with reduced pollution.[11]

GNP and Well-Being

A third weakness in the link between growth and pollution, as usually stated, concerns the measurement of production. If increasing human well-being, rather than increasing GNP as it is now measured, is taken as the measure of

[10] Allen V. Kneese, Robert U. Ayres, and Ralph C. D'Arge, *Economics and the Environment: A Materials Balance Approach* (Baltimore: Johns Hopkins Press for Resources for the Future, Inc., 1970).

[11] For the use of energy, the picture is less clear. Recycling materials involves the use of energy, either in the form of human labor or in the form of combustion, electric power, or other non-human force. Recycling does not seem to offer ways of reconciling increasing production with reducing energy use. Technologies designed to increase efficiency or reduce pollution in energy capture and use might be possible. Without them, possibilities for recycling are very limited.

growth, then this kind of growth might be more compatible with environmental protection. Several economists interested in environmental problems have criticized the measurement of Gross National Product on this score. Even the Net National Product, which is computed by deducting depreciation from GNP, is not truly "net." It includes consumer goods which will increase welfare, but also includes goods used in self-defeating cycles of competitive consumption that increase nobody's well-being. Military powers spend large amounts on hardware to keep up with each other: billions of dollars later they are still stalemated (and everyone agrees it would be even worse if one were ahead); different producers increase their spending on advertising and packaging to maintain their shares of markets; consumers are forced into similar races to maintain their status. Other examples are less obvious. Individuals and companies spend more and more on legal services, so the people they sue must also hire more lawyers. Legislators fear the poor will cheat the treasury, and add more and more accounting requirements to requisites for receiving poverty program funds. This increases the cost of the poverty program. Commuters flee further to the suburbs to escape the city; when enough have done this, the city's congestion is repeated in the suburbs and they must flee again.

A number of economists argue that these expenditures that do not increase well-being should be deducted from GNP, to approximate a measure of the economy's positive effects on people's lives. Others would deduct depletion of the environment along with depreciation of man-made equipment, in computing NNP. On the other hand, GNP is criticized for omitting many nonmarketed activities that do add to well-being. Economists used to mention, as a curiosity, that the measured GNP would fall if a man married his cook and ceased to pay her a salary. But a very large part of the productive effort of society—including most of the work of child rearing—takes the form of unremunerated labor by wives. That the measurement of GNP may reflect the low prestige of "women's work," is no defense of GNP as a true measure of well-being.

Kenneth Boulding has argued even further against the concept of GNP. Since GNP measures effort in production, and not the ability of consumers to benefit, it might be called the "Gross National Cost." He characterizes the GNP measure, and all of economics, as assuming that

> economic activity is a throughput, a linear process from the mine to the garbage dump . . . the real measure of economic welfare is not income at all. It is the state or condition of the person, or of the society. Income is just the unfortunate price that we have to pay because the state is corruptible . . . consumption is decay—your automobile wearing out, your clothes becoming threadbare. It is burning up the gasoline. It is eating up the food. Consumption is a bad, not a good thing; production is what we must undergo because of consumption.[12]

[12] Kenneth E. Boulding, "Fun and Games with Gross National Product: The Role of Misleading Indicators in Social Policy," in H. W. Helfrich, Jr., *The Environmental Crisis* (New Haven: Yale University Press, 1970), pp. 157–70.

GNP, or the replenishing of the stock of goods, is at best a rough measure of potential welfare. More efficient recycling, conservation, and use of the stock of goods and resources might increase well-being with a lower measured GNP. An ecologically viable increase of welfare, without increases in GNP as now measured, or with some increases accompanied by a change in the input-output mix, is clearly a logical—and perhaps a technological—possibility. But the issue of GNP measurement also points to an unhappy possibility; that growth of production and pollution may occur without increases in human well-being, a possibility discussed further in Chapter 7.

SOCIAL COST AND EXTERNALITY

These considerations show that increased levels of material consumption and well-being might be compatible with lower levels of resource depletion and pollution. But growth, in fact, has led to considerable pressure on the capacity of the environment to absorb wastes and provide materials. To argue that growth of a less destructive nature is possible, it is necessary to argue that the institutions of the economy have led to more waste than is necessary, and that other institutions could reduce waste and increase well-being. Economists have developed a number of arguments and concepts which are used to explain and to evaluate the decisions that people and organizations make about resource use, and the systems of institutions that affect these choices.

Underlying these analyses is a concept of *social cost*, the loss to society as a whole, as a result of some activity. This cost may be measured either in terms of *opportunity cost* (the value that the resources used up in the process could have provided to society in other possible uses) or in terms of *disutility* (psychological costs of doing the work and foregoing other resource uses). As has been stated in the introduction, the economist terms an activity justifiable if this social cost is less than the social benefit the activity brings about; and recommends carrying out only that amount of the activity as will equate marginal benefits and costs.

In most economic activities, the participating decision makers generally look only at those costs directly relevant to themselves as producers. They will consider the cost of their labor in terms of its disutility to them, or its possible wage in other activities. They will evaluate other resources as their market price, or at the price they could implicitly command in some other use. Economists recognize, of course, that these may not be the only costs. Other production may be reduced by pollution or resource depletion which comes about as a side effect of some activity. Or, there may be direct costs imposed on people outside of the productive process, by the noise, pollution, or other aspects of the production. Economists usually define the social costs of production as including all of these direct and indirect costs. Sometimes, however, they will reserve the term only for the indirect costs, when it is necessary to remind people that these costs exist but have not been taken into account by decision makers.

Economists sometimes try to determine, using the notion of social cost, exactly what the best level of activity and of waste disposal (or pollution) in certain industries might be. Some of these efforts, and the problems involved in their implementation, are discussed in subsequent chapters. Much of the work of environmental economics, however, has been to show how the economy is structured to leave some costs of resource depletion and waste disposal out of individual decision makers' calculations. Many of these explanations center on the institutions of property rights and market allocation of goods and some resources.

Three alternative perspectives have been developed, which give possible explanations of why, with economic growth, the economy may waste resources, overproduce pollution, and disrupt the balance that exists between humanity and nature. One theory (that of external diseconomies in the use of common resources) holds that imperfections in the application of property rights are at fault, but that these imperfections can be corrected. A second position is that social costs are so pervasive that, in a developed country, property rights cannot be adjusted to make decision makers take account of all costs. A third position holds that environmental problems and social costs stem from basic power relationships in society that underlie the system of property rights, so that the system itself is at fault.

Common Resources and External Diseconomies

The first explanation centers on the idea that in a market economy, most but not all resources may be privately owned. Although land belongs to the landlord; mines, to the claim owners; laboring ability, to the workers; and machinery, inventories, and other goods to the capitalists; the air and perhaps the water have no exclusive possessors. In this situation, each private owner will try to use the absorptive capacity of air and water because it is free, and the resources may be overused.

The overuse of "free" resources is generally defined with reference to a standard of what would happen if all resources were owned. This is the assumption that economists usually make in discussing the operation of a theoretical "perfect" market economy. In such an economy, economists have often argued that marginal social costs and benefits will be equated, and activities whose costs exceed benefits will be weeded out, by the workings of market competition.

This result—the action of what Adam Smith termed the "invisible hand" —depends on several conditions, which make each producer of a good bear all of the costs of production by having to purchase all of the factors used in production. The producer considers producing at all possible levels. He compares the marginal cost of each additional unit of output with the additional revenue it will bring in. If the economy is "perfectly competitive," this increase in rev-

75

enue will be equal to the price of the good, which will be equal to its value to the consumers who freely choose to buy it at that price. If the conditions of the model of perfect competition are met, marginal cost will be equal to marginal benefit for each line of production. If total costs exceed total benefits, the good will not be profitable to produce at all. Finally, competition among producers requires each to use the least expensive technology. The economy will have automatically reached the optimal level of production, given the existing distribution of resources among owners. Few economists believe any real market economy will behave exactly as the theory predicts; but, even those who generally believe the market works well admit to some circumstances under which it will produce an amount of pollution that is greater than it should be, and a use of natural resources that goes beyond the optimum rate.

The argument is the same one that has already been encountered in considering common fields in agriculture. For the market to work effectively, each producer must take into account all of the costs his activity imposes on the economy. His private cost must equal social cost. But, if some resources are not owned by the producer, or purchased, or rented, by him at a market price, this will not be the case. If he can use a pasture free, or use water with no cost to himself, or use minerals which are available at less than the cost of production, he will be able to increase profits by overusing these resources. They will be used even though the benefits from production are less than the costs. Similarly, if the producer can reduce his costs by dumping wastes into the environment in a way that causes damage to others, he will do so if he doesn't have to pay for the damage. Economists define these social costs that are not reflected in private cost to the producer as *external diseconomies*. If these are not included in production costs, again the total benefits of production may be less than total costs in a market.

More technically, the concept of externalities is usually extended to include both *external economies* (benefits that do not accrue to the decision maker) and *external diseconomies* (costs that are not borne by the decision maker). They can also be divided into pecuniary and technical externalities.[13] *Pecuniary externalities* are those increases and decreases in cost which are transmitted through the market mechanism to *third parties* with whom the decision maker has no direct market relations. For example, if the decision maker is a buyer of products, and his purchase of a good allows his supplier to take advantage of economies of scale, other third party buyers from the same supplier may have their costs reduced. These pecuniary external economies are particularly important in the development of momentum in the early stages of economic growth. Pecuniary external economies and diseconomies may also arise from firms' and households' decisions of where to locate within modern cities. One

[13] Tibor Scitovsky, "Two Concepts of External Economies," *Journal of Political Economy*, Vol. 62, April 1954, pp. 143–51.

party's move may increase or decrease the cost of transport or public services to others.

Technical externalities are those in which the connections are not made through the market at all. The firm that emits smoke in producing goods for one consumer, may affect others who buy nothing from it. Because a common resource that does not enter into the market can be the transmitter of the external effect (the air carrying the smoke in this case), many external diseconomies result from the existence of common resources. Producers, in general, will tend to impose external costs on others (or, overuse common resources) because they do not have to bear the social costs involved.

The link between common resources and technical external economies makes it clear that the definition of externalities is dependent on a system of property. If, for example, a stream belongs to a landlord, he may charge people for the use of the water, either for consumption or for its waste disposal properties. Presumably, he would not allow use of the water if the user did not cover the cost involved. If the water is unowned, then anyone can attempt to use it. People may make use of its waste disposal properties even if this prevents consumers (who would be willing to pay more if a landlord were auctioning off use rights) from drinking it. Because resources are available free, they are overused. Pollution reaches levels that no longer are tolerable. The market, in these cases, has failed to direct production with an effective invisible hand.

Many economists have argued that the reason for environmental damage during economic growth is that this growth made it necessary to ration what had been unowned common resources. If so little waste is being put into a lake that the natural processes of degradation remove the wastes, then it does not matter that the lake is unowned. But once effluents exceed the limit that the lake's oxygen supply can degrade naturally, then overuse of the common resource begins to have a cost. In a sense, these economists argue, the institutions of ownership have lagged behind growth: it is necessary to complete the system of property by naming owners (or, some equivalent of owners) for all resources as they become scarce.

According to this argument, if a way could be found to make air and water into property, their owners could rent their use. Competition between those seeking to rent air for smoke disposal and those renting it to breathe, would establish an equilibrium price. The most efficient level of use would result. Of course, there is no way of turning the air into individual property without giving it all to one individual. Each particular piece of air cannot be identifiably separated from other pieces, the way flour can be bundled into individual sacks for use or sale. Giving all the air to one profit-seeking owner would create a monopoly, which would also prevent the market from finding the proper level of air use. However, there may be some institutions which would allow an equivalent to ownership, in that they would result in the same price being charged for air use that would result under competitive private ownership. These methods might include auctions by the government of "rights to pollute," charges on those whose pollution did cause damage, and other public controls, as well as (in some cases) combining of ownership of different properties to remove the externality (as in the case of court orders that polluters buy downwind properties if they intend to continue emissions.)

A number of those methods for replacing property rights with an equivalent are considered in the next chapter. The essential point of all of them is an assumption that the market will work to allocate resources efficiently, except for the effects of a finite number of imperfections or common resources. These imperfections, it is argued, can be corrected by specific policies. Economic growth, in this view, requires the introduction of these new policies, but if this is done, private property and the market can still be used as basic economic institutions.

Pervasive External Costs

Patching up the market through a system of property right equivalents may be sufficient for efficient resource use according to some economists, but not all would agree. Some have argued that economic growth has made social costs, and particularly those that operate through effects on the environment, so pervasive that a system of property rights could no longer be constructed which would make the invisible hand function properly. Ezra Mishan and Karl Kapp, particularly, have raised this argument. They doubt that with so many materials circulating in the atmosphere and the stratosphere; in rivers, lakes, and oceans; in underground water tables, in the soil, and in the bodies of wildlife; that all resources ever could be made into private property for use in market transactions. How hard it would be for an "owner" of the air to know which users of materials to charge for what amounts of pollution damage. But if not *all* resources can be made into property, there is no proof that making more resources into property will yield a better result than leaving fewer resources as property. This is an application of a complicated argument in advanced economic theory called the *theory of the second best* which holds that if markets for several factors in an economy are imperfect (that is, they do not equate marginal benefits and marginal costs), then making one more market perfect will not necessarily move the economy toward a better position, even if making all markets perfect would yield the best outcome.[14] If, for example, water is made into property, and a perfect market for the waste disposal properties of water is created, this will make sewage disposal more costly to the individual producer of garbage. But, because many wastes can be burned, instead of dissolved, and carried off in sewers, air pollution may increase if the air is not also made property along with water. The theory of the second best states that there is no way of knowing (unless the exact response of everyone can be measured ahead of time) whether

14 Kneese, Ayres, and D'Arge, op. cit., pp. 87–107.

imposing property rights to water, but not air, will make society better or worse off.

Kapp argues this invalidates the entire idea of achieving efficiency through the market:

> As soon as one passes beyond the traditional abstractions of neoclassical price analysis and begins to consider the neglected aspects of unpaid social costs it becomes evident that the social efficiency of private investment criteria, and hence the alleged beneficial outcome of the allocation process under conditions of private enterprise, is largely an illusion. For, if entrepreneurial outlays fail to measure the actual total costs of production because part of the latter tend to be shifted to the shoulders of others, then the traditional cost-benefit calculus is not simply misleading but actually serves as an institutionalized cloak for large scale spoliation.[15]

The argument of Karl Polanyi is similar to that of Kapp, except that Polanyi goes farther by including the benefits of stable social communities, along with the use of air and water and basic biogeochemical cycles, among the things that cannot be made into property. Polanyi argued that there were disastrous consequences to making part of society into a commodity (labor), that could be moved about by the result of price changes; and by making part of nature into a commodity (land), whose uses could be altered by similar price changes. Rapid changes in prices led to the rapid migration of labor from place to place, and to drastic changes in land use. Villages were abandoned, cities grew too large, stable social relations were impossible, and natural resources were destroyed for short-term gains. In each case, it could be said that behavior, in response to the market, was imposing both social and environmental external diseconomies. Polanyi's belief was that the attempt to run the economy by a self-regulating market was a utopian experiment that failed. Society, he argued, would have to take charge of the economy again to prevent disaster; the replacement of market forces by planning was necessary, with the only question being whether the planning should be democratic or dictatorial.[16]

Some objections to Polanyi's argument can easily be raised. He claimed the market was destructive because it was a "self-regulating mechanism," not controlled by society. But ecologists find that natural ecosystems are often stable because they *are* self-regulating mechanisms. The Tsembaga of New Guinea survive because population is limited and dispersed by a self-regulating mechanism. Defenders of the market argue that it too, could become such a benign and stabilizing mechanism *if* all resources really were given prices. What would be required, in their view, is replacing all common resources by property. However, if recent economic growth has made the flow of materials in the environment so complex and, potentially, so costly that property rights can no longer

---

[15] K. W. Kapp, *Social Costs of Business Enterprise* (Bombay: Asia Publishing House, 1963), p. 271.

[16] Polanyi, *op. cit.*

effectively be placed on everything, then Polanyi's basic argument about the consequences of the market and its basic irreparability may hold, now, or in the future, even if it did not hold for the nineteenth century period he considered.

The third basic perspective on market institutions and the environment holds that even if everything were property, there would still be a strong tendency for the economy to impose excessive social costs. Indeed, private property over productive resources, in this view, is at the very heart of the problem. The perspective has its roots in the nineteenth century economic analyses of Karl Marx, but it can be modified, to apply to ecological problems that arose as capitalist nations became more developed.

For Marx, the workings of a capitalist system ensured that workers would only be paid a socially defined subsistence wage; that wage at which they could support themselves and their families to the point at which a new generation of workers would be produced. Because businesses were always able to cut costs by substituting new equipment for labor, thus throwing workers out of work, the functioning of a labor market would always drive the wage back to this subsistence level, below which nobody could work. Workers, in turn, had to participate in this market because they had no alternative sources of income. After the enclosures had removed them from agriculture they had no *means of production* of their own: no resources with which to earn their subsistence other than the labor power they could sell to the capitalists for the wage. In return for this wage, Marx wrote, the capitalists could extract from the workers enough work to cover not only the workers' subsistence wage, and the depreciation on equipment (the paying back of investment in earlier machine-making labor), but also a normal business profit.

The subsistence wage and the amount of work that could be done in a day were not, however, biologically determined levels. Rather, Marx said, they depended on the state of a continuing *class struggle* between the workers and the capitalists. As a group, the workers sought to determine a minimum below which it was socially unacceptable to live, and to put limits on the length and intensity of work on the job. On their part (although they were also competing with each other), the capitalists would seek to reduce the subsistence cost and extend the acceptable amount of a day's work. The market mechanism, given the distribution of property that put all means of production in the hands of the capitalist, would ensure that these socially defined limits of subsistence and endurance would apply to each worker.

Within this bargaining situation, Marx placed much of his emphasis on working conditions and hours of labor. In *Capital*, he described the nineteenth century factory environment at great length. He chronicled cases of death from overwork; accidents occurring when workers were overtired from twelve, fourteen, and even twenty hour shifts; poisoning of match factory workers from phosphorus; adulteration of foods; high death rates among potters, blacksmiths, and child laborers.[17] Any of these conditions can be seen as a passing off of social costs by business onto the workers. For any wage rate, a faster work pace cuts business costs, and makes the worker bear these costs through worsened conditions. These costs are a form of social cost—and a form of pollution. As one union put it, in a recent advertisement on "Earth Day," "Pollution: turn of the century—they called it the sweat shop."[18] These were social costs shifted to others by the employers, but the reason was not that some resource was nobody's property. If the manufacturers had officially owned the stale air in the shops, nothing would have been different.

Working hours have been shortened considerably since Marx's day, and working conditions have improved, perhaps by more than Marx anticipated. Whether these improvements were the result of economic development alone, or whether the gains had to be wrung from the capitalists by the political action and strikes of labor unions, is a matter of debate. Clearly, however, the acceptable minimum wage and the maximum extent to which working conditions and hours can be stretched by employers are much improved (from the workers viewpoint) since the nineteenth century. Nonetheless, within factories, pollution and unsafe working conditions still remain a form of social costs often borne by workers. 14,000 Americans a year die in industrial accidents; many more are incapacitated.[19]

Many of these costs have attracted attention in recent years. Pesticides harm grape and lettuce pickers; dust and gas in mines cause black lung disease to the miners; cadmium poisoning does permanent damage to the nervous system of workers in some factories. In earlier times, mercury poisoning caused madness in hatters who used the material to treat furs, and hand painting luminous watch dials with radium caused cancer in factory workers. These are cases of particularly severe damage; a factory that is merely smoky may cause lesser damage to workers on the job and in homes near the factory. Removal of these hazards, presumably, would increase the cost of the products, reducing the profits of management or raising the price to consumers. As long as the costs can be imposed on the workers instead, owners (or consumers) will benefit, perhaps by less than the workers suffer.

This would appear to be a case in which the imposition of social costs by the capitalists continues to occur (to some extent at least), irrespective of the completeness of the property system. Indeed, if the air and water were made into property—but the property of those who were already capitalists—it is hard to see how the social costs imposed on workers would be reduced.

Some economists have argued, however, that if workers know that certain types of work are dangerous, or even just dirty, they will refuse to accept these jobs unless they are paid enough to compensate them for the special risks and damage. If this is true, a factory manager would have to compare the costs of

[17] Karl Marx, *Capital* (1887) (New York: International Publishers, 1967), Vol. 1, Chap. 10, p. 15.
[18] "International Ladies Garment Workers Union," *New York Times Magazine*, April 19, 1970, p. 45.
[19] Ray Davidson, *Peril on the Job* (Public Affairs Press, 1970), p. 1.

reducing local pollution, or correcting the unsafe conditions, with the costs of attracting workers to those factories if conditions continue to be bad. This should, in principle, lead to the most tolerable level of damage if labor markets are perfectly competitive. Sometimes, it appears that risky jobs in fact do pay higher wages to attract workers. Test pilots and astronauts are given high pay, and the army knows it will have to raise its pay if it wants to attract enough volunteers to do without the draft.

In many cases, however, workers cannot insist on higher pay for risky jobs, through individual market activities. Individual workers often cannot know all of the risks in a job unless their employers tell them. What is more, some workers have a limited choice of jobs because of low educational levels, the need to remain in some region where there are few jobs, racial discrimination, or a general economic recession. Moving, going back to school, or changing the overall economic level may be beyond the means of the worker. Thus, he must choose, not between a risky job and a safe job at lower pay but rather between the risky job and no job. The result is that risky, and dirty, jobs are often also the lowest paying jobs—those that the workers with least chances in life must suffer.[20]

What is more, if all factories impose pollution costs on their workers, then there may be no possibility of avoiding damage by changing jobs, or of receiving differentially higher wages for higher risk. Unless the damage is sufficient to actually reduce the number of workers in the whole economy, employers as a group can impose damage on their workers. The same argument can be extended to at least some types of pollution that occur outside of factories. If companies, as decision-making units, find that the quality of life does not enter into their balance sheets, and if individual company directors, by virtue of personal wealth, are the most able in society to escape pollution by buying homes in better suburbs or by investing in air conditioning and vacations, then companies can cut costs by imposing pollution on the working public in general. Thus, specific pollution may itself be a form of imposing costs on workers by capitalists. Stopping the pollution, like cutting working hours and making conditions at the plants safer, would appear to be the task of organization by the workers as a group, in opposition to the capitalists. Making the air into the property of existing property owners (or of the government, which, Marx argued, would be controlled by business) would not help.

SUMMARY

The growth of economics in history has allowed production to reach a point at which depletion of resource supplies and pollution have become seri-

[20] Lester Thurow and Robert Lucas, *The American Distribution of Income: A Structural Problem* (Washington: Joint Economic Committee, 1972), pp. 47–50.

ous problems. Table 4–2 summarized some of these problems. Some writers claim that these environmental problems are inevitable results of growth in GNP or material living standards. They argue that zero GNP growth is the only alternative to environmental decay. Several arguments may be made against a rigid adherence to this view. Not all activities entering into GNP create equal amounts of effluents or use equal quantities of resources. Current methods of production, even in the most destructive sectors, may be improved by recycling or other new technologies. Finally, not all growth, as now measured, contributes to human welfare. There may be kinds of selective growth which could increase well-being without environmental destruction.

This raises the question of why growth is not more selective. These are alternative views of the institutional arrangements in a market economy with private property which could lead decision makers (businessmen) to impose social costs of environmental disruption on the public. Each of the three views tries to explain why, with growth, a market system may lead to increasing pressure on the environment, including pressures created which do not bring anyone benefits to outweigh the costs. In the remaining chapters, the approaches to correction suggested by the three views will be discussed. Chapter 5 begins with a discussion of the first view, that the system of property rights is incomplete, but can be perfected.

Selected Readings

The relation between growth and pollution is explored in Warren A. Johnson and John Hardesty, *Economic Growth vs. the Environment* (Belmont, Cal.: Wadsworth, 1971), and Henry A. Jarrett, ed., *Environmental Policy in a Growing Economy* (Baltimore: Johns Hopkins Press for Resources for the Future, Inc., 1966). Economic theory of externalities is presented further in E. S. Mills, "Economic Incentives in Air Pollution Control," in M. I. Goldman, *Ecology and Economics* (Englewood Cliffs, N. J.: Prentice-Hall, Inc., 1972), pp. 142–48. The basic presentations of the role of pervasive externalities are Karl Polanyi, *The Great Transformation* (Boston: Beacon Press, 1957); Karl William Kapp, *The Social Costs of Private Enterprise* (New York: Shocken, 1971); and E. J. Mishan, *Technology and Growth: The Price We Pay* (New York: Praeger, 1970). The simplest exposition of Marx's position is probably *Wages, Prices and Profit* (1865), in K. Marx and F. Engels, *Selected Works* (New York: International Publishers, 1970), pp. 186–229. A. V. Kneese, R. U. Ayres and R. C. D'Arge, *Economics and the Environment* (Baltimore: John Hopkins Press for Resources for the Future, Inc., 1970); *Study of Critical Environmental Problems, Man's Impact on the Global Environment* (Cambridge, Mass.: M.I.T. Press, 1970); and *Cleaning Our Environment: The Chemical Basis for Action* (Washington, D. C.: American Chemical Society, 1969) are important sources on economic and scientific aspects of the problems of waste disposal.

Environmental

Fine Tuning

There are several proposed methods for equating the marginal costs and benefits of economic activities when environmental pollution is involved. Most seek to reduce the incentive for one decision maker to impose external social costs on others. The methods include governmental regulation, compensation payments, effluent taxes, bribes, subsidies, and mergers. Many economists present them as operating within a situation in which markets are achieving a generally acceptable pattern of activities, except for a few distortions caused by the existence of common resources. If, however, there are many, pervasive externalities disturbing the market, or if monopolies or other factors prevent the operation of an invisible hand, use of these methods may amount to "trying to fine tune a system that is getting more and more out of focus."[1]

In this chapter, the concepts used by economists for measuring the costs and benefits of different levels of pollution are defined and illustrated. Next, proposed methods for removing externalities and *fine tuning* pollution are surveyed. Finally, some problems are considered that may make the proposed methods fail. These include differences of measuring costs and benefits, and political problems arising when external damage or environmental control affect different groups unequally.

[1] Allen V. Kneese, Robert U. Ayres and Ralph C. D'Arge, *Economics and the Environment* (Baltimore: John Hopkins Press, for Resources for the Future, 1970), p. 119.

COMPARING COSTS AND BENEFITS

No human society can avoid pollution entirely. Keeping warm and cooking food, as a very minimum, requires fires; agriculture involves some runoff of materials. Too much pollution can lead to disaster. Somewhere in between may lie a most tolerable or *optimal* level of effluent discharge, justified by the usefulness of the polluting activities and by the costs that would be required to carry these on with less pollution. A first problem for economists who approach ecological issues is the determination of the tolerable level of pollution for a society. Only then can they ask what economic institutions may lead to excessive levels of pollution or may help to limit pollution to the best levels.

Defining the Most Tolerable Level

One requisite for a level of pollution to be tolerable is that it not lead to the destruction of society, either by poisoning the inhabitants or by destroying their sources of food and materials. This requirement of viability is not unique to economists. Ecologists pose the question for any population, human or non-human, of whether it can survive in its environment. Economists, however, have some additional criteria to define a tolerable level of pollution. These often cannot be applied without considerable help from biological scientists and without knowledge of what people in society consider as valuable. Sometimes, they cannot be used at all. Sometimes, however, they can provide a method for some choice as to what level of pollution, among those that permit survival, is most desirable.

The economist enquires whether some level of pollution is tolerable by comparing its costs and benefits. The benefit from a level of pollution is the value to people of the product that requires that level of pollution. The cost is the damage imposed on the environment and other people. When more than one process can be used to make a product, then the costs and benefits of two processes can be compared. The cost of one process compared with another means of making the same product is the additional expense of running that process. The benefit is the reduction in pollution damage involved. For an activity to be tolerable, its benefits must be greater than its costs, including pollution. What is more, no alternate means for giving these benefits must be available that that would reduce pollution costs by more than the additional production costs involved in using it.

Even if these conditions are met, the economist may not consider an existing level of pollution as most tolerable or optimal. *Only that level of pollution at which the excess of benefits over costs is greatest meets this test.* An example can show what is required. Fig. 5–1 represents the total costs and the total benefits from the burning of different amounts of coal. Both costs and benefits

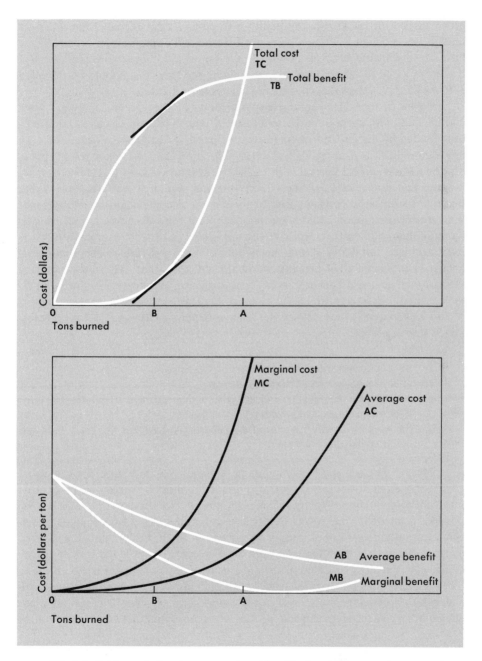

FIG. 5–1 Total, marginal, and average costs and benefits of combustion.

increase as coal consumption increases, but benefits grow more rapidly at first (as people heat their homes and travel, yet the air is not overburdened). Later, costs grow more rapidly, as energy is used for less essential products, and the air grows thick with smoke. At any point up to point A, the excess of benefits over costs is greater than if no coal were used. Faced with an either-or choice of one level of combustion between O and A, society would choose consumption. But if there is a choice of any level of combustion, the level that should be tolerated is B. At this level, the excess of benefits over costs is greatest.

Figure 5–1 restates the argument in terms of average and marginal costs and benefits. The average is the total cost of benefit at some level of consumption divided by the amount of coal used. At point A, the average benefit of each ton used equals its average damage cost. The marginal cost, or marginal benefit, of each ton of coal burned is the addition to total cost, or total benefit, from burning that many tons *instead of only one ton less*. It is the effect of adding that one more ton to consumption. If, for a level of combustion, marginal benefit is greater than marginal cost, burning one more ton will increase total benefits by more than total costs. It will increase the excess of benefits over costs towards its maximum. Similarly, if one more ton of coal will create marginal costs greater than its marginal benefits, it should not be burned. The intersection of the marginal cost and benefit curves come precisely, and necessarily, at point B, the consumption level at which the excess of benefits over costs is greatest.

The economist thus defines the *most tolerable*, or *optimal*, level of pollution as one at which:

1. the population will not be destroyed
2. total benefits are greater than total costs
3. no alternate method is available that would add less in production costs than it would take away from pollution costs
4. the level of activity for the method chosen is such that marginal costs and marginal benefits are equal

Measuring costs and benefits may be difficult. Not only must the ecological effects of the pollution be determined, but a value must be placed on these costs that can be compared with the benefits produced. Sometimes, this may be impossible. Sometimes, the effects of different pollutants in the environment, which come from different sources, cannot be sorted out scientifically. Sometimes, costs and benefits accrue to different people or businesses. Even if the money values of the gain and loss to different people can be compared, there is no certainty that the worth of a dollar is the same to all individuals, who may vary in wealth and habits.[2] Sometimes, also, the benefits and costs of some level of pollutant emission may themselves depend on the other economic activities going on in

---

[2] When the costs of a system to be evaluated will not all be made at the time the system is installed, some method of adding future costs to present costs is required. Simply adding up the amount of money required in every future year would, however, overestimate the cost. An initial investment, deposited in a bank or invested in government bonds, will provide for the annual costs at less initial expense. This sum, which must be invested to cover the future expenses, is called the discounted present value of these expenses and is the most appropriate figure to use in calculating the costs of any investment.

society. These problems must all be kept in mind when deciding whether any calculation of costs and benefits is valid.

A Case of Measurement

Despite difficulties, costs and benefits of pollution or of its removal have been measured in some cases. More measurement studies are undertaken every day now that environmental pollution has been perceived as a problem. Some of the first measurement efforts concerned water pollution. Data exist over long periods of time for rates of flow of rivers and for the amounts of different chemicals and organic materials entering at different municipal and industrial waste discharge plants. This information can be used to estimate the effects of pollution abatement strategies.

There are several possible strategies that can be used for water pollution control. Some involve seasonal or year-round increases in stream flow, through storage of water or diversion of other streams. Others require a reduction of wastes entering the river, either through treatment of sewage or reduction of activities in areas drained by the rivers. The effects of different possible strategies can be calculated through the use of computer models of stream flow. Estimates of the rates at which wastes are degraded, at different levels of concentration and different rates of stream flow, are made. Then, the computer is used to calculate the amounts of waste passing different points in the stream, under different assumptions of the amount of water entering the watercourse and the levels of effluents discharged at different points. If the costs of different methods of reducing waste emission and of augmenting stream flow are known, then it is possible to calculate the method of lowest cost for reaching some given level of cleanliness. (Cleanliness may be expressed in some measure such as parts per million of oxygen left in the water after organic wastes are degraded.) Finally, the benefits of each level of purity may be estimated and compared with costs.

One such study was undertaken of the Delaware River that considered water pollution abatement to different levels of cleanliness.[3] At the cleanest level, level one, the water would be safe for swimming at all points. At the intermediate levels, swimming would be possible at some points not immediately downstream from towns or industries, and fishing would be possible in selected locations. At level four, boating for recreation would be possible but swimming and fishing were ruled out. At a minimally tolerable level, level five, the river would merely be preserved from becoming septic and creating a hazard to riverside activities.

The study calculated the costs of achieving the different levels of cleanliness under several assumptions. Under one assumption, waste treatment was required at all points at a uniform level: no more than a certain concentration of wastes could be discharged at any point. Such a strategy would be the simplest

[3] Allen V. Kneese and Blair T. Bower, *Managing Water Quality: Economics, Technology, Institutions* (Baltimore: Johns Hopkins Press for Resources for the Future, 1968).

to implement, through a uniform code of treatment requirements applying to all locations. But it would also be a costly method, because some wastes would be treated artificially that the stream itself could have degraded naturally. A second assumption, that a zoned system of waste treatment plants be used, also was tested. It would take advantage of the natural treatment properties of the stream. Finally, strategies involving both waste treatment plants of different sorts at different points and stream flow augmentation at seasons of low flow also were considered. For all levels except level one, at which all points on the river were to be safe for swimming, the mixed strategy of zoned treatment and stream flow augmentation proved less costly than reliance on treatment plants alone. For maintenance of the river at level five, only seasonal stream flow augmentation was estimated as necessary. The estimated costs are presented in Table 5–1. The figures given include the initial costs of treatment plants and water retention dams to regulate seasonal flow, plus an initial financial investment which would yield annual dividends sufficient to cover the annual cost of maintaining the system in operation.

The benefits of attaining different levels were estimated by a variety of methods. Level five was the easiest. To allow the Delaware River to become a stinking sewer would involve the waste of billions of dollars of property along its banks. In Table 5–1, level five is used as a benchmark, with the loss of at least a billion dollars entered as a *negative benefit* if nothing were done. Indeed, the cost of not attaining level five might be considered infinitely large, if it is unthinkable not to provide for at least that level of cleanliness.

Cleanliness beyond level five will not affect riverside investments. The benefits of this greater cleanliness must be sought elsewhere. One possible benefit might be cleaner water for municipal water supply or for industry. The authors

Table 5–1 COSTS AND BENEFITS OF POLLUTION ABATEMENT

Abatement Level	Total Costs			Total Benefits[2]	
	Uniform Treatment Only	Zoned Treatment Only	Cost Minimizing Method[1]	High Estimate	Low Estimate
none	0	0	0	∞	−1000
5	—	—	30	0	0
4	130	80	65	280	120
3	155	120	85	310	130
2	315	250	215	320	140
1	460	460	460	350	160

Source: Computer estimate for Delaware River in A. V. Kneese and B. T. Bower, *Managing Water Quality* (Baltimore: Johns Hopkins Press, 1968). Figures in billions of dollars.

[1] Mixed stream flow regulation and treatment plant arrangement giving lowest costs to attain that level.

[2] Positive benefits are recreational benefits. Negative benefit at level with no abatement represents destruction if stream becomes septic.

of the study found few benefits would arise from use of cleaner stream water for these purposes. At any level, water would have to be treated for these uses. But cleaner water would allow boating, fishing, and swimming in different locations.

The value of these recreation benefits is difficult to estimate. It is not known precisely how many people would use recreational facilities of different kinds. Estimates are made on the basis of figures from comparably sized cities and towns with public recreational facilities and on the basis of use of existing private and more distant public facilities. Even if use can be estimated, placing a value on it is difficult. When facilities are provided free, or at an admission fee not set by competitive supply and demand, the economist cannot assume that price represents what the facilities are "really worth" to consumers. The best that can be done is to make some estimate of what people are willing to pay for existing private recreational facilities or in transport expenses and time in reaching more distant parks. The projected use of the new facilities is evaluated on that basis. Various assumptions can be made as to whether with increased use of facilities their price would fall, as price usually falls in a competitive market with increased supplies. Thus, estimates of total benefits are necessarily only guesses, and the investigators of the Delaware presented two alternative estimates, which are shown in separate columns of Table 5–1.

With total costs and benefits estimated, it is then possible to compare marginal costs and benefits of different levels of abatement. This is done in Fig. 5–2. The two estimates of benefits are graphed along with the estimate of costs using the cost-minimizing effort for each level of control as selected by the computer program. For each level, the figure graphed is the additional cost or benefit of reaching that level instead of the next dirtiest level. As the figure shows, the marginal benefits are clearly greater than the marginal costs at going from no treatment to level five and from there to level four. If the higher benefit estimate is used, it is also worth investing to achieve level three. On the other hand, the additional cost of 20 million dollars to achieve level three would not be worth the additional benefits of only 10 million if the lower benefit estimate is used. (This is so, even though the total benefit of 130 million is still greater than the total cost of 85 million to attain this level: level four remains more economical under this assumption.) Even using the highest benefit estimate, reaching level two adds more to cost than it adds to benefits. The study thus shows that pollution control to attain level four—and perhaps level three—is warranted. Control measures sufficient to reach levels two and one and make most of the river available for swimming, would be too costly.

The Delaware River pollution study indicates the kind of measurement that will increasingly become available for the policy maker. The information will always depend on assumptions—such as those made about the demand curve for recreation in this study. But, because alternative assumptions can be used, it will sometimes be possible to use these studies for narrowing down the range within which the most tolerable level of pollution can be said to occur. In this

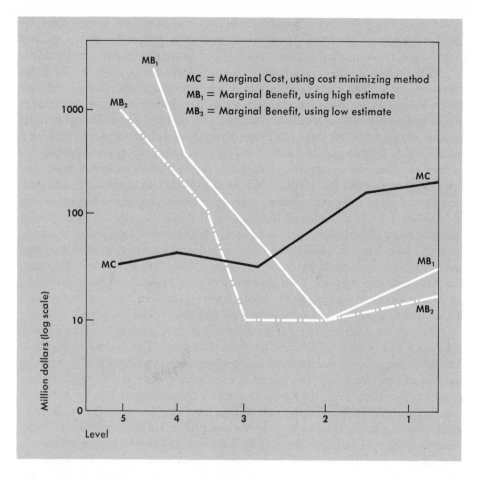

FIG. 5–2 Marginal costs and benefits of pollution abatement. (Delaware River figures, from total costs and benefits in Fig. 5–1.)

case, to know that it may be either level four or three is to know more than that either boating or swimming might be possible in a cleaner river, but at an unknown cost.

INSTITUTIONS TO CONTROL EXTERNALITIES

If the costs and benefits of some form of pollution control can be estimated, society can attempt to bring emissions to the most tolerable level, or to establish an optimal level of abatement. Sometimes, as may be the case with sewage treatment prescribed in the Delaware Study, this will require government spending on treatment facilities. Sometimes, however, it will also be necessary to affect the actions of other groups who are imposing external damages on others. Those doing the damage may be private businesses, individuals, or even other governmental bodies. As was discussed in the last chapter, they may pollute or cause damage to others because they do not have to bear the costs of the damage.

In principle, any of several institutional arrangements can reduce external damages. Direct regulation or prohibition, charges or legal liability for damage, subsidy or bribes to avoid damage, and merger of the interests of polluters and their victims are all possible mechanisms that may help to limit effluents to the level where marginal costs and marginal benefits are equated. Their usefulness in different situations may vary because of problems in their implementation and because of different effects on the distribution of costs and benefits. If users of the facility contribute to, and suffer from, pollution unequally, the regulatory institution chosen will affect who bears the cost of abatement or of damage done by the pollution remaining at the most tolerable level. The different methods will be discussed using the case in which the polluter and the person bearing the cost of pollution are different individuals and in which the costs and benefits of possible controls have been measured.

Regulation and Prohibition

Fig. 5–3 shows the marginal cost curve for a method of pollution control. The costs of attaining each additional unit, or level, of cleanliness may include

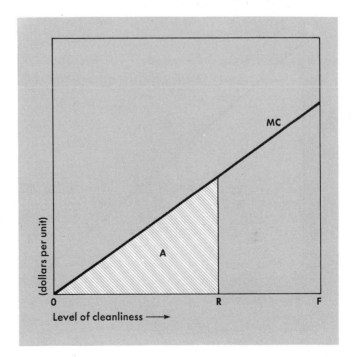

FIG. 5–3 Marginal cost of reducing pollution. Area A is total cost of reducing pollution to cleanliness level R, part of way to pollution-free level F.

both the direct costs of abatement activities or equipment and the costs imposed by reducing levels of production that cause pollution. For example, costs of reducing air pollution include expenses of producing cleaner gasolines and automobiles with cleaner-burning engines, plus possible costs to drivers from a reduced speed. Because the curve shows marginal cost, total cost for reaching each successive level of cleanliness equals the sum of the marginal cost of getting to that level from the next lowest level plus the costs already involved in getting to that previous level. Geometrically, the area under the marginal cost curve, up to the level of abatement reached, represents total cost.

Similarly, Fig. 5–4 represents the marginal benefits of pollution abatement. The benefits may include the possibility of new activities or a reduction in costs of undertaking old activities. In the air pollution case, benefits might include both a reduction in cleaning and medical bills and the benefit to consumers from increased use of parks which might be made more attractive by cleaner air. Once again, the total area under the curve, from the left, or zero, axis up to the point of abatement actually reached, represents the total benefit. Similarly, the area under the curve to the right of the point actually reached, represents the benefits foregone by victims of pollution because it exists.

In Fig. 5–5, the two curves are combined. The general principle is applied that the most tolerable level of pollution is that which gives the greatest excess of total benefits over costs. This is the level at which marginal costs equal marginal benefits. In the figure, this is level Q. If the government regulates pollution

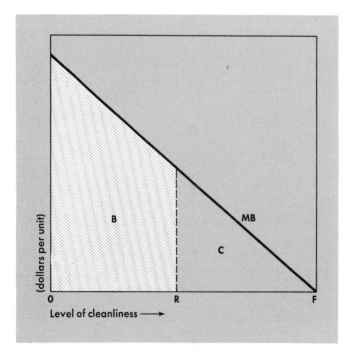

FIG. 5–4 Marginal benefits of reducing pollution. At cleanliness level R, area B is total benefit compared with original level of pollution (zero cleanliness); C is cost of remaining pollution.

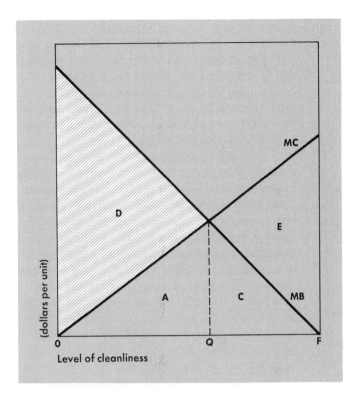

FIG. 5–5 Costs and benefits of regulation. Area *D* gives net benefits of reduction to level Q. Remaining damages are given by *C*; costs of additional reduction to pollution-free level *F* would be C + E.

emissions to this level, area *D* will give the net benefits of a reduction of pollution to this level. It is equal to the difference between the total benefits of reduction to level *Q* (area *B* in Fig. 5–4) and the total costs of reduction to the same level (as in area *A* in Fig. 5–3).

That this is the most tolerable level of pollution can easily be seen. At any lower level of cleanliness, the net benefits would be less than area *D*. At a higher level of cleanliness, net benefits are also lower. Suppose, for example, that the government tries to prohibit all pollution. It may decide to do so because the original regulation, which brought pollution down to cleanliness level *Q* still left pollution in the air with a total cost of *C*. However, if the government does ban all pollution, polluters will have to bear the cost of an increase in cleanliness to level *F*. The total cost of this additional reduction of pollution is given by the area under the marginal cost curve between points *Q* and *F*. This total is represented by the sum of areas *C* and *E*. In other words, area *E* represents the excess of additional costs over additional benefits from a reduction of pollution from the *Q* level to the *F* level.

The reduction of pollution to level *F* is thus not a reduction to the most tolerable level. Some amount of pollution is warranted by a comparison of benefits and costs of reduction. Of course, if the only policies government can con-

95

sider are either a total prohibition of pollution or no action at all, then the total ban will be preferable to inaction as long as area D is greater than area E. In Fig. 5–5, as drawn, this is the case; total benefits from a reduction to the pollution free level slightly exceed the total costs of that reduction. But this will not be the case for all combinations of cleanup costs and benefits. Sometimes, a total ban may be worse than no action at all. Generally, it will be more costly than a selective prohibition, which seeks to hold the level of pollution as close to level Q as possible.

A selective regulation is not easy to devise and enforce. Government authorities often define maximum acceptable levels of pollution. When pollution approaches that level, legislation may allow the declaration of an emergency. Some activities may be closed down, and others, reduced in scale. If the community knows which sources of pollution are most expendable, they can reduce damage in the way that has the lowest marginal cost. For example, during a temperature inversion, automobiles might be prohibited from entering a downtown area at rush hours unless they hold four passengers. Car pooling, enforced that way, has some marginal cost, in bother to the commuters, but it is not a very high cost. Or, in the case of a water shortage (not a form of pollution, but an environmental problem), the sprinkling of lawns, the washing of cars, and the use of water using institutional air-conditioning systems may be restricted.

Under more normal circumstances, however, there may not be a common agreement as to the lowest cost method of reducing damage. An across-the-board reduction of all effluents by a uniform percentage may interfere with high priority services as well as with luxuries that can be dispensed with at low cost. In such a case, the cost of reduction to each level is greater than that given in Fig. 5–3. More specific regulations might impose quotas on the pollution that different individual users or kinds of users can emit, but these obviously involve difficult political problems. If many industries, towns, and individuals contribute to pollution, each party will claim that others should reduce their effluents, so that the tolerable level can be reached. The definition of the safe level of pollution itself may be subject to political controversy. Nonetheless, in some cases of apparent danger, such as the use of DDT in high quantities, government has imposed prohibitions and regulations to reduce use.

Compensation Liability Requirements

An alternative method to limit external diseconomies is a requirement that those causing damages must compensate their victims. One method for this is to allow victims to sue for damages. Such a system might induce individual parties to pollute only up to the most tolerable level. If polluters know they must compensate victims, they will themselves calculate the cost of a reduction in pollution and compare it with the amount they stand to save in reduced damage claims. The reduced damage claims will, themselves, be a measure of the benefits of reducing pollution. Thus, additional expenditure on control will be made if the additional benefits it generates are greater. Equality of marginal costs and marginal benefits will be induced.

This outcome is shown in Fig. 5–6. The producers of pollution will spend money to reduce pollution to point Q, but not beyond. Reduction to point Q is warranted because the cost of reduction, area A, is less than the payments that will be made otherwise, areas $A + D$. On the other hand, it is cheaper to pay the compensation given by area C than to bear the cost, $C + E$, of reducing pollution further. The similarity of Fig. 5–6 to Fig. 5–5 shows the equivalent results of compensation and control, as far as the total level of pollution is concerned.

However, there is one fundamental difference between the two results. In the case of regulation, the cost of pollution that still exists at level Q is borne by its victims. In the case of compensation, that cost is borne by the polluters and whoever causes damage will be the one to pay for it. This principle seems to make compensation a more equitable system, in terms of some sense of fair play, or a requirement that groups or individuals take responsibility for their own actions. Whether it is more equitable in another possible sense—that of contributing to equality in income—will depend on the relative wealth of pollution victims and of those who either pollute or can buy consumer goods more

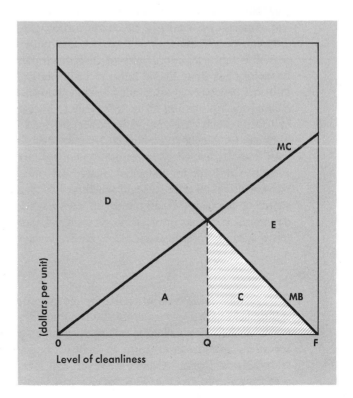

FIG. 5–6 Compensation payments. The polluter elects to risk payments given by area C because it would cost C + E to avoid the damage, but he spends A to avoid risk of having to pay D + A.

cheaply because their producers pollute. Compensation will lead to greater equality than regulation if the pollution remaining at level Q is caused by a yacht that fouls the source of a poor fisherman's income. It will increase inequality in the case in which a poor fisherman's outboard leaves some oil on a country club beach.

One additional benefit sometimes claimed for a compensation principle is that it reduces the need for a bureaucratic apparatus to enforce controls. Each possible polluter will himself calculate the damages he may inflict and evaluate the benefits from pollution against possible legal claims. A government office will not have to do the job. This will not necessarily reduce the number of necessary calculations. A large number of different producers of the same pollutant may have to repeat calculations that could be done once by a government agency. What is more, if the work of the executive branches of government is reduced, the job of the judiciary is made more difficult. Not only will judges have to rule on the extent of damages in the myriad cases in which they do take place, they may also have to rule on lawsuits brought by individuals who are in fact not damaged, but who sue nonetheless, hoping to win something in the process. Although some people have a higher opinion of the wisdom of judges than that of bureaucrats, this is not universally true. Shifting opinions about the United States Supreme Court show that judicial control, like any other form of control, can involve controversy.

Judicial enforcement of compensation can be extremely difficult if many different individuals are involved as either polluters or victims in the same process. It is impossible to determine how much damage each particular automobile or factory has done to the lungs of each particular citizen during a smog alert. It would be extremely difficult for each individual near an airport to assess the damage each particular airline has done to his ears and nerves. If each individual had to sue each other individual, the case load in courts would be prohibitive. This can be alleviated somewhat by laws that allow groups of victims to bring joint lawsuits, called class actions, against groups of polluters. Even then, however, it is difficult for judges to decide how much each polluter should have to pay into the total damages and whether victims are entitled to equal or unequal shares of the claim. Requirement of compensation payments, enforced through the courts, can thus provide an efficient and equitable means of regulating external damage in some cases, but be ineffective in other cases.

Voluntary Compliance, Bribery, and Subsidy

Even without administrative or judicial controls, some forms of pollution will be held to the most tolerable level voluntarily, if victims are allowed to enter into contracts with polluters, paying them to stop imposing damages. Some conservatives advocate this form of control as avoiding government interference with individual rights. Others, however, call it bribery. That it may work can be seen by returning to Fig. 5–6. In this case, it will be worthwhile to the victims for them to offer a payment of the amount given by area A, or, if necessary, any amount between A and $A + D$, to the polluter if he will limit pollution to level Q. In this case, the bribe will be greater than, or at least equal to, the polluter's benefit A from increasing his pollution further. But it will be less than the cost that the victims would bear if cleanliness were O. On the other hand, a further bribe to increase cleanliness from Q to F is not possible; the benefit C to the victims is less than the bribe of $C + E$ that they would have to pay to induce the polluter to clean up further.

Thus, the ability to bribe a polluter into voluntary compliance may limit pollution to the most tolerable level. But the effects on the distribution of benefit will be the reverse from those in the case in which compensation is paid by the polluter. Instead of making payments of C, the polluter receives a bribe of some amount ranging from A to $A + D$. (The exact amount of the bribe depends on his bargaining power, because any bribe between the two amounts is mutually beneficial.) This result may be more or less equitable from a viewpoint of equality than the result in the compensation case, depending on whether the polluters or the victims are wealthier, but it violates many people's ideas of fairness in a way that compensation payments do not.

Bribery involves another problem. If it becomes a widespread custom, people may threaten to pollute in order to collect bribes to desist. Unless prohibited legally, false threats of pollution could become a profitable form of blackmail. Regulating such threats could be a more difficult judicial problem than the evaluation of damages under a compensation rule.

Similar difficulties apply to offering public subsidies to polluters who reduce their effluents. Firms may adopt pollution-causing methods of production in order to receive rewards later for reducing damages. Even if this form of waste or corruption is avoided, subsidies for reduction of existing pollution will mean a transfer of benefits to the former polluters from the taxpaying public and appear to reward polluters for their past sins. If polluters are relatively wealthy, it will also increase inequality.

Nonetheless, there are circumstances in which subsidy is defensible. Taxes can be levied progressively (even if governments do not always do so). Polluters may not always be wealthy, and the companies that pollute may sometimes provide jobs in otherwise depressed areas or sell inexpensive necessities to nonaffluent consumers. What is more, polluters may not always be to blame for the damage they do. They may, in fact, have begun operations at a time when their emissions were not recognized as dangerous. Or, given the waste disposal capacity of the environment, their emissions may not have been dangerous at first. Only with increased population or activity in surrounding areas have some forms of pollution begun to strain the disposal capacity abilities of rivers and airsheds. In such cases, subsidies may be equitable in the sense of not punishing the innocent and not burdening the poor.

Whether subsidies are "fair" in either of these senses, or whether they are adopted as a last resort because polluters are too powerful to be induced to

99

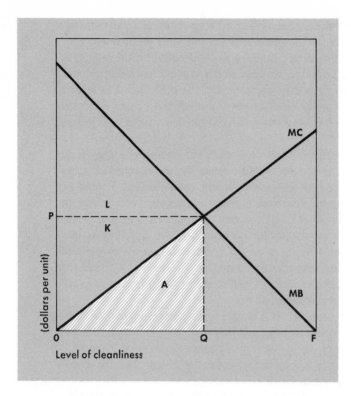

FIG. 5–7 Subsidies for eliminating pollution. A subsidy of A, or any greater amount less than the amount given A + K + L, pays the former polluter as much or more than it costs to reach cleanliness level Q. If a constant figure P per unit of new cleanliness is paid, the subsidy is given by area A + K.

clean up by any other means, government payments to those who reduce pollution can be designed to achieve optimum pollution levels. This is shown in Fig. 5–7. Any subsidy greater than, or equal to, area A, will make a cleanup to level Q worthwhile for the polluter; as long as the subsidy is less than the area $A + K + L$, it is worth giving.

The subsidy may also be offered in the form of a bonus of a certain number of dollars per unit of cleanliness achieved. For example, a certain sum may be offered for each percentage point by which the amount of oxygen in a lake is increased or the concentration of sulphur dioxide or carbon monoxide in the air is reduced. In this case, assuming the contribution of a particular polluter to the reduction can be identified, the subsidy should be set equal to the marginal benefit of a one unit increase of cleanliness at Q, the most tolerable pollution level. The polluter will have an incentive to increase cleanliness as long as his marginal cost is less than the per unit subsidy, but not beyond that point, and will himself select Q as the level of cleanliness to be attained. In Fig. 5–7, P is the per unit subsidy, and the total subsidy paid is given by the area $A + K$.

Government can regulate external diseconomies by taxing as well as spending. By charging fees for the use of environmental waste disposal capacities or for such facilities as parks that can become congested, it can deter their use. By charging users of normally free natural or public facilities, the government puts itself in the place of an *owner*, charging a price for their use. This price, if set properly, can induce an efficient level of utilization. The fees collected can be used to compensate the victims of damages resulting from use of some environmental facilities or to replace other taxes as a source of general revenues.

A number of these fees have been discussed by economists, under different names. Fees for the use of water or natural park land have been urged, to prevent depletion of supplies or congestion of the wilderness beyond the point at which costs passed along to consumers would exceed the benefits reflected in their willingness to pay. *Congestion tolls* for highways and other transport facilities have been suggested, as a means of making each user pay the equivalent of the cost his presence imposes on other users. *Effluent charges*, or taxes on the discharge of wastes into the air or water, have been suggested to deter pollution. Like compensation payments, these fees are held to be "fair" in that a polluter, or other user of a service, must bear the cost. Like the other methods of environmental regulation already discussed, they can be used to hold pollution to its most tolerable level, as well as to limit use of other facilities to the level at which marginal costs equal marginal benefits.

In Fig. 5–8, a tax of *P* dollars per unit of discharge is assumed to be levied.

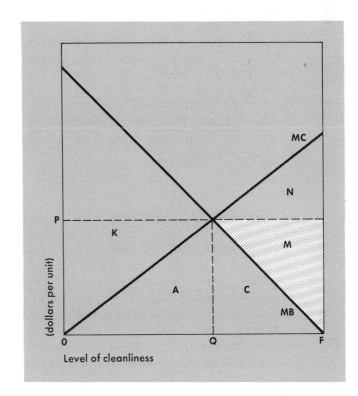

FIG. 5–8 Effluent charges. A tax of P per unit of discharge will induce the polluter to reduce pollution or increase cleanliness from zero to Q, because the cost of cleanup A is less than the tax bill A + K. For the remaining pollution, the polluter pays a tax of C + M rather than pay C + M + N to achieve a pollution-free level F. After compensating victims in the amount given by area C, the government has M left over for general revenue purposes.

The amount P is set, equal to the marginal cost or benefit of a unit of cleanliness (a reduction of pollution by one unit), at the most tolerable level Q. The polluter will prefer to reduce emissions rather than pay the tax, as long as the cost of cleaning up is less than the per unit tax; thus, he will reduce pollution up to the level of cleanliness Q. However, he will not reduce pollution beyond that point, because to achieve greater cleanliness, the marginal cost would exceed the per unit effluent tax avoided. Thus, the polluter will end up paying a tax of P per unit of pollution still emitted at point Q. This tax is given by $M + C$ in Fig. 5–8. If the government compensates the victims of the remaining pollution, giving them the amount shown by area C, it will have M left over to add to its general revenues. It may use this money to lower other taxes or perhaps to subsidize the reduction of pollution in other areas where subsidies are appropriate.

Like compensation payments, effluent charges have their proponents as a method of pollution control worth using on all occasions. However, they have drawbacks in some circumstances. Like regulation and all of the other possible institutional methods of control, a system of taxes on externalities requires the government to have the political strength to impose control and the knowledge of pollution to determine the marginal costs and benefits of different levels of cleanliness or pollution. The tax rate of P, that is, must be calculated before the tax is levied. What is more, as conditions change in the economy the tax rate may have to be changed. This is no more of a problem than is the computation of damage payments by judges under a system of compensation, but it is not easier. Of course, the government may try to approximate the exact levels of costs and benefits in different circumstances by applying one per ton rate to some kind of discharge in all locations. This would mean missing the most tolerable level, but it might involve a more tolerable level than presently prevails under many circumstances. Finally, there may be cases in which an effluent discharge would weigh too heavily on low-income individuals to be advisable from a social viewpoint. But, although effluent discharge fees are not universally applicable, they do appear to be one form of environmental fine tuning with possible wide application.

One final method of environmental control also may be applicable at times. This is the merger of the interests of polluters and victims. If polluting firms and their victims merge, the result is what economists call an "internalization of the external diseconomy." Put simply, the effects that previously were ignored by polluting firms, because they affected only others, must now be taken into account because they affect the joint firm's own profits. Mergers have sometimes been forced by outright prohibitions of some external economies. For example, firms that pollute surrounding farms may elect to buy out the farmers if prohibited from damaging crops or livestock with their wastes. This purchase is economical if the marginal cost of cleaning up would be greater than the cost of buying out the farmer who has complained of the pollution. In such cases, the effect of the purchase is similar to that of compensation payments as far as the ultimate level of pollution and the distribution of costs. The pollution continues, but the former farmer receives the purchase price. However, if, as sometimes happens, the polluter acquires the farm at a price lowered by pollution, compensation is incomplete. Although mergers are sometimes practical, however, they often may require the creation of such large companies that the result would be a monopoly that is undesirable for other social and economic reasons. For example, if an electric power company were required to own all of the homes in the area affected by its smoke, it might have to be landlord over an entire city.

TECHNICAL LIMITS TO FINE TUNING

The institutions described in the preceding section are designed to be substitutes for property rights to the environment. Pollution involves the use of the absorptive capacity of the environment in an attempt to disperse or recycle wastes. Because the environment is not owned by a landlord, "airlord," or "waterlord," individuals and firms are not charged for its use, even if their effluents impose social costs on others. Because costs are external to his calculations, a polluter will use the common resources of the environment to excess. The different methods proposed (apart from regulation) seek to remedy the situation by charging the polluter for the damage he does to each other individual in society. Thus, he will consider all of the social costs of his use of the environment as private—money costs in making his decisions on what to produce or emit, and marginal costs will be held to the point at which they are matched by marginal benefit.

Can these institutional arrangements end the overemission of pollutants? Some economists think they can; they argue for effluent charges, for codes governing compensation payments, or even for an "air exchange" to facilitate the purchase of rights to use the air for waste disposal and to allow the orderly payment of subsidies or bribes for nonpollution. Other economists disagree. They argue that although the methods proposed can internalize some externalities and eliminate some pollution problems, they can not adequately ensure that pollution as a whole will be held to the most tolerable level—or even to a level that will ensure survival. Several different limits to the use of these fine tuning measures have been suggested.

Measurement Problems

Charges, subsidies, even regulation designed to equate marginal costs and benefits require that the costs and benefits of different levels of emission be quantified. This requires, however, that scientific knowledge of the physical ef-

103

fects of different emissions be available and that the social cost of these effects be measurable in money terms. These requisites are often not met. The interaction of different pollutants in the atmosphere and in the ocean is only beginning to be known. Research in these areas is a high priority task, but nobody can be sure how fast knowledge will advance. Models that could describe accurately the marginal effect of one factory or one freeway full of motorists are not easily developed. Yet, a system of compensation payments may require not only that the effect of each emission on total levels of pollution be known, but that the effect on separate classes of victims be determined.

Even if the effects of different pollution levels on physical damage can be known, the attribution of costs may be difficult. For example, a statistical comparison of cities finds that higher levels of sulfate and particulate pollution are associated with increased death rates. In particular, sulfate pollution can be associated with mortality from cancer and heart disease, and particulate pollution with tuberculosis and asthma. The authors estimate that a 50 percent decrease in air pollution might increase life expectancy by three to five years.[4] But what is the cash value to be placed on this increase? Is it just the additional amount people could produce if they lived three years longer and the savings in medical costs brought about by better health? Or are there additional benefits? Using court claims in accident cases to estimate the cost of shortening a life is only to substitute the guesses of judges for that of economists. There is no "true" answer.

Another study compares house values in polluted and unpolluted neighborhoods. It finds that otherwise equivalent houses in different parts of one city sell for $87 to $250 less for each .25 mg/100 cm² of daily sulfation content in the air.[5] But is this study measuring the total cost of air pollution on the assumption that homebuyers will pay exactly as much more for a house with cleaner air as they would lose by living in a dirtier atmosphere? Or is the market only reflecting some of the costs in the difference in values? Unless there is some independent source of information on costs, the economist does not know if he is measuring the cost of pollution, or the realism of consumers in their own guesses at the cost.

In both cases, what is more, only some pollutants have been measured and correlated with health or house prices. Would reducing sulfation alone have the benefits predicted by the equations? Other pollutants might actually cause some of the damage attributed to sulfation. Would a reduction in sulfation accompanied by an increase in nitrogen oxides make things better or worse? The statistics do not say.

Exact measurement is not always necessary for policy making. In the case of such persistent pollutants as nondegradable insecticides (DDT), heavy metals

[4] Lester B. Lave and Eugene P. Seskin, "Health and Air Pollution," in P. Bohm and A. V. Kneese, *The Economics of Environment* (New York: St. Martins, 1972).

[5] R. G. Ridker and J. A. Henning, "Determinants of Residential Property Values with Special Reference to Air Pollution," *Review of Economics and Statistics*, Vol. 49, No. 2, May 1967, pp. 246–56.

(lead and mercury), and some radioactive materials (Strontium 90 before atomic tests were banned), emission levels obviously exceed tolerable levels. Only when discussion can be centered on what emergency uses (radioactive isotopes for medical purposes; DDT to control epidemic diseases) may be warranted as most tolerable pollution, will exact cost-benefit comparisons be needed. Even if taxes on lead in gasoline are used to reduce emissions, they will be based on a need to survive or an obvious conclusion that total costs exceed benefits, not an exact calculation that marginal pollution costs equal the amount of the tax. This is necessary "gross tuning" perhaps, but not the fine tuning promised by the clarity with which Figs. 5–3 through 5–8 are drawn.

Relativity of Ceteris Paribus Measures

Fine tuning will also be illusory in some cases because the measured costs and benefits of different levels of pollution may depend on changeable features of the economy. The marginal cost of operating a car may depend on whether a factory nearby is operating, on whether elderly people with lung diseases live nearby, or on the direction of the wind. The benefits, in turn, may depend on the availability of alternative forms of public transportation or on the value of speed between two points. In such cases, quantifying costs and benefits is only possible on what economists call *ceteris paribus* assumptions. These are assumptions that most of the world cannot be changed and that the policy or level to be discussed must be determined "all other things being equal." In the language of the chapter title, this means that these calculations are only possible on the assumption that environmental controls will, in fact, only be fine tuning. Thus, in the Delaware River study, the calculations are made on the assumption that the number of people and industries in Philadelphia and the other metropolitan areas on the Delaware River will grow at currently estimated rates, irrespective of the need for pollution control. Similarly, the study of St. Louis air pollution takes the population of the city and its demands for energy as given. If, in these studies, costs of making the air free of sulphur, or the river apt for swimming, appear to outweigh the benefits, the pollution is determined to be economically tolerable only "other things being equal." If the population of the United States were dispersed into small towns instead of concentrated in big cities, the costs and benefits of pollution control would clearly be different.

Similarly, as will be discussed in Chapter 6, if costs and benefits of restricting automobile use are calculated on the assumption that people live in suburbs without subway connections, the studies may show it to be too costly to clean up the air. On the other hand, if the possibility of mass transit and changes in housing location are included in the analysis, the result may vary. However, the policies required to reorient the residential and commuting patterns of cities go far beyond what an air pollution control agency alone could enforce or what could be accomplished with bribes, compensation rules, or effluent charges.

These limits to fine tuning imposed by *ceteris paribus* assumptions may

105

hold even if everybody suffers equally from pollution. They become worse when polluters and victims are different groups. In these cases of nonreciprocal externalities, the method of fine tuning itself may change the background variables held constant in determining costs and benefits. This may actually change the most tolerable level to which pollution is to be adjusted.

This occurs because different distributions of cost or income under the different institutions of control may affect the amount of benefit or cost. Suppose a smoky factory is ruining the park of a poor neighborhood. If a system of bribes is permitted, the neighborhood may not find it worthwhile to pay the factory to reduce its emissions. With people short of money, and working long hours, they will find it more important to save their money than to pay for a cleaner park. If, however, the rules are changed and the factory is required to pay compensation to smoke victims, the potential income of the neighborhood is raised. If the factory continues to belch forth smoke, people will receive compensation payments. They will work less overtime and have more desire for leisure at their new, higher, income. The value of the park to them may go up— in which case an accurate measure of benefits would require that the factory raise its compensation payments and cut its emissions still further. With compensation, the level of pollution that results will be lower than with bribery. But both will be most tolerable levels under their respective institutions, because, in each case, the marginal costs and benefits of further reduction will be equated.[6]

Interconnectedness and the Second Best

Further problems arise from the complex interconnections that occur between different forms of emission. Not only do different emissions interact with each other in the air or in water, they also may be substituted for each other by polluters. Thus, the controls placed on one form of pollution may lead to increased costs from some other form of pollution, as when a firm, barred from dumping solid wastes, burns them and fouls the air. Or controls on one form of pollution may reduce costs from another, as when reduced emission of nitrates or phosphates into a lake, by reducing algae growth, allows natural degrading of other organic wastes. In this case, the costs from untreated municipal sewage dumping will be reduced. Still further interconnections may occur between pollution control and the tightness of oligopoly control in some industries. If, for example, pollution standards make it harder for new companies to compete with established coal mines, the price of coal may be raised to a monopoly level.

When any of these interconnections occur it is not certain whether improving controls over one pollutant—to equate its measurable marginal benefits and costs—will make things better or worse off for the society as a whole. This is a case of the general theory of the second best, mentioned in the previous chapter. Perfect markets in all materials may keep pollution and production at optimal

[6] E. J. Mishan, "Pangloss on Pollution," in Bohm and Kneese, op. cit.

levels, at least given the income distributions. But perfection of some markets while marginal costs and benefits remain unequal in others is not always an improvement.[7]

POLITICAL LIMITS TO FINE TUNING

All of these technical and measurement problems show how difficult it is to determine what institutions could allow the achievement of a most tolerable level of pollution. But, even if that level may be described in theory, the actual design of institutions may be impossible in practice. If externalities are nonreciprocal, so that some polluters gain from shifting costs to society while others lose, pollution control will involve conflict. Even in cases of purely reciprocal externalities there may be difficulties in achieving the optimum level of control.

Conflict with Nonreciprocal Pollution

The possibility for conflict where polluters and victims are separate groups is obvious and can be illustrated by some historical examples. These show, frequently, that controls are adopted when the victims are more powerful than the polluters and are avoided when the polluters are more powerful. In neither case is there a guarantee that the political process yields an optimal amount of control.

Two cases involving externalities in mining operations may be contrasted. The first is California gold mining. Most people assume that the gold rush ended when the miners ran out of gold. Strictly speaking, this is not true. There is still gold in the ground in California. True, the easily collected nuggets were all removed and the gold dust was panned from river sands by the early prospectors, but more gold remained in the ground. Miners continued to dig gravel from the hills and sift it for gold. This source of gold still remains, but miners no longer search it out. The reason they have stopped is not the difficulty of finding gold; it is the cost of getting rid of the gravel.

The first prospecting companies could simply dump the gravel in the nearest river. Water would wash it downstream, leaving the miners room to dump more gravel. Downstream, these tailings might block the rivers, but, at first, nobody objected to the floods this caused because much of California was still uninhabited. Then, farmers moved into the central valley, took advantage of the fertility of the land and prospered. Eventually, they became more powerful than the gold miners in the California legislature. Because floods were affecting their farms, they enacted a law to prohibit the dumping of mine tailings in streams. Gold mining was not banned. But the miners were prohibited from imposing

107

[7] R. C. D'Arge and E. K. Hunt, "Environmental Pollution, Externalities and Conventional Economic Wisdom: A Critique," *Environmental Affairs*, Vol. 1, No. 2, June 1971, pp. 266–87.

external costs on the farmers (or the rivers). The high cost of disposing of the gravel by loading it into carts or trains made mining unprofitable. The gold rush was over.

Strip mines for coal in Appalachia also leave behind a residue of tailings. Earth, rock, coal dust, and other materials are swept into streams and destroy the surrounding farmland. In this case, however, the coal companies are more powerful in state politics than relatively poor farmers, who suffer the damage. The state regulations for strip mining that are passed are ineffective. Although Appalachian farmers, like those in California, would like a ban on all environmental damage, they do not have their way. Bribery by the victims to influence the legislatures or to buy off the coal companies directly is not possible, because the victims are too poor. Those who lose their farms generally have to leave the region and frequently end up as welfare recipients in urban areas outside the coal-mining states. Thus, even the city governments that suffer some of the eventual costs cannot influence the strip mining laws which are passed by other states.

That the legislative outcome was optimal is shown in neither example. The costs to farming from floods in California were probably more than the value of the gold that could have been produced. If mines were required to compensate farmers for damages rather than banned completely from leaving tailings, they might have closed anyway. The legislature's action does not prove this, however. Similarly, it may be that cheap coal is more advantageous to society than agriculture or recreation in Appalachia could be. But the legislature's failure to pass strong laws does not prove that this is the case. That coal companies impose uncompensated externalities shows that local residents are losing and coal companies and coal consumers are gaining. But which side gains or loses more is not indicated by the legislative decision to let the situation continue.

Interest group pressure does not always lead to nonoptimal decisions. Two successful regional environmental programs—the reduction of air pollution in Pittsburgh and of water pollution in the Ruhr valley in Germany—were promoted by major businesses of the areas. They saw environmental control as preserving their investments in the long run. The rest of the public may have benefited although they were not the principal organizers. Public concern for the environment led to government action in the face of interest group opposition in some other cases, including the treaty prohibiting atmosphere nuclear testing and the removal of subsidies to supersonic transport plane development.

Environment as a Public Good

If externalities are reciprocal, so that everyone loses by pollution, or if, at least, a majority are victims, pressure for public control policy may be more effective than when victims are a limited group. Economic growth may make such a consensus more likely. As economies develop, more people can afford luxuries, and environmental amenity may be among these luxuries. With more people desiring a clean environment, they may be more willing to vote government money (paid for by their taxes) for cleaning the environment or bribing polluters to reduce effluents. They may vote for controls even when those will increase the prices of consumer products. Polluters may find it harder to avoid controls by bribing only enough of the population to win a majority, thus compensating only the "least expensive" 51 percent of the victims for damage. However, even when everyone may gain something by limiting pollution, political problems may impede control.

The reason lies in the nature of environmental protection. To some extent, it is what economists call a "public good," a product or service that can be enjoyed by people who do not buy it.[8] Reducing air pollution makes people's lungs cleaner, irrespective of whether or not they have contributed to the cleanup effort by paying for sulphur-free fuel, planting green shrubs, or contributing to environmental defense funds. There is no way of charging the users of cleaner air by denying the benefits to noncontributors, in the manner that most goods can be withheld from those who do not buy them. Thus, clean air and other public goods cannot be provided for sale in a market by profit-making businesses. They must be provided by a government that makes everyone pay his share in taxes.

If more people come to desire environmental improvement, they may vote for these taxes. If everyone expected the results to be equally beneficial, felt the weight of taxes equally, and expected his fellows to pay taxes that were levied, then voting might lead directly to the optimal level of government expenditure. Each person would vote for taxes up to the point at which his contribution to another dollar's worth of cleanup equaled his benefit from the additional effort. (Marginal cost divided by population would equal marginal benefit divided by population.) This best outcome is, to be sure, not guaranteed.

At the very least, each taxpayer may try to avoid payment as far as he can, expecting to enjoy the benefits of other people's taxes, whether he pays or not. Preferences of different people for different kinds of public goods may lead to an inability of any program to receive a majority of votes—or, conversely, to a situation of logrolling in which too many programs are adopted. Taxes may fall unequally on different members of the population, leading to conflict over programs even when total benefits clearly exceed total costs. Finally, if experience leads people to mistrust government, they may expect taxes to be wasted, and oppose any proposed programs. All of these factors can lead to underspending on public goods from the viewpoint of the population as a whole.

SUMMARY

This chapter discussed several different institutions that may hold external diseconomies to their most tolerable level. This is the level at which marginal costs of control equal marginal benefits of damage reduction. Direct

[8]Paul A. Samuelson, "The Pure Theory of Public Expenditure," *Review of Economics and Statistics*, Vol. 36, No. 4, November 1954, pp. 387–89.

provision of public damage-reducing facilities by the government, regulation and prohibition, requirement of compensation payments, bribes and subsidies for pollution reduction, effluent charges and other tax incentives, and requirements that external effects be internalized through mergers can all limit pollution to tolerable levels under certain conditions. These prerequisites include both a political ability of the public to impose the institution and the measurements or general knowledge needed to determine the appropriate level of control. However, the different institutions may have very different effects from each other in terms of the distribution among people of the costs and benefits of control and thus in terms of their "fairness." What is more, all of these controls are instituted, and their levels calculated, taking many conditions as given. They are fine tuning, given the distribution and size of total population and the overall economic institutions of a country.

The general argument for fine tuning, and some cases in which it worked, are presented in Marshall I. Goldman, *Ecology and Economics: Controlling Pollution in the 70s* (Englewood Cliffs, N. J.: Prentice-Hall, 1972), and T. D. Crocker and A. J. Rogers III, *Environmental Economics* (Hinsdale, Ill.: Dryden, 1971). Further considerations are presented in J. M. Dales, *Pollution, Property and Prices* (Toronto: University of Toronto Press, 1968); R. M. Coase, "The Problem of Social Cost," *Journal of Law and Economics* Vol. 3, 1960, pp. 1–44; Harold Demsetz, "The Exchange and Enforcement of Property Rights," *Journal of Law and Economics*, Vol. 7 1964, pp. 11–31; and Francis M. Bator, "The Anatomy of Market Failure," *Quarterly Journal of Economics*, August 1958.

Measurement issues and cost-benefit analyses of specific programs are presented in Ronald G. Ridker, *Economic Costs of Air Pollution* (New York: Praeger, 1967); Paul Downing, *The Economics of Urban Sewage Disposal* (New York: Praeger, 1969); Azriel Teller, "Air Pollution Abatement: Economic Rationality and Reality," in Roger Revelle and Hans M. Landsberg, *America's Changing Environment* (Boston: Houghton-Mifflin Co., 1970), pp. 39–55; and several studies published for Resources for the Future, Inc.: A. V. Kneese and B. T. Bower, *Managing Water Quality* (Baltimore: Johns Hopkins Press, 1968); J. C. Meadley and J. N. Lewis, *The Pesticide Problem* (Baltimore: Johns Hopkins Press, 1967); G. O. G. Lof and A. V. Kneese, *The Economics of Water Utilization in the Beet Sugar Industry* (Baltimore: Johns Hopkins Press, 1968).

Legal issues are explored in James E. Krier, *Environmental Law and Policy* (Indianapolis: Bobbs-Merrill, 1971).

The Social Organization

of Internal Combustion

CHAPTER SIX

Gasoline combustion by automobiles is one source of pervasive externalities in urban areas that marginal adjustments cannot regulate effectively. Charging for each engine's marginal contribution to smog damage will not bring costs and benefits into balance. Because of chemical reactions in the atmosphere, individual damages are hard to measure accurately. Total damage sometimes may not be affected by changes that reduce some effluents. Controls powerful enough to reduce internal combustion significantly would, however, raise so much political objection as to be impossible.

The objections seem justifiable from an economic perspective. Many urban areas allow few alternatives to automobile use. Land use patterns have developed presuming the predominance of auto transport. Separation of cities and residential suburbs, the unavailability of mass transit, and lack of government support for alternative transit modes make the automobile a necessity of life. Taxing the automobile user would place a heavy fiscal burden on the public, without significantly reducing pollution. The economist must agree that unless the entire transportation system is reorganized, the benefits to each driver from access to work, shopping, and recreation may be greater than the individual automobile's addition to pollution costs.

Although each motorist may be justified in driving, given the available alternatives, the entire system may still be irrational. Indeed, a city with several million drivers rationally choosing to use their engines may become uninhabitable. Replacing the present organization of cities by a more compact settlement pattern with good public transit might allow an equivalent standard of living with less pollution. Analyzing automotive pollution requires considering not only the limits to fine tuning, but also the social and economic organization of cities, transport systems, and energy supply. The principal question is what forces limit the options open to residents, giving them little alternative but to contribute pollutants to the air. This chapter examines the institutions of urban life and the political economy of the petroleum industry in light of this question.

LIMITS TO INDIVIDUAL INCENTIVES

Automobiles and Effluents

Automotive exhausts are the largest source of air pollution in the United States. Tables 4–3 and 4–4 show household automobile use accounts for nearly one-third of all petroleum use. Cars, trucks, and other transportation equipment account for 23.6 percent of all energy consumption (measured in British Thermal Units) and automotive engines represent 95 percent of all of the installed horsepower capacity of prime movers. Motor vehicles emit 60 percent of air pollution (measured by weight), including most of the carbon monoxide, half the hydrocarbons, and almost half of the nitrogen oxides in the air (See Table 6–1). The transport of petroleum to its consumers also causes ecological problems, including oil slicks from tanker accidents and damage to tundra environments from heat required to keep oil flowing in arctic pipelines.[1]

Cities are particularly affected. Normally, the atmosphere disperses pollutants, which are eventually recycled by natural processes. Emissions in congested areas, however, may accumulate more rapidly than natural dispersal can remove them. They form pollutant clouds within which chemicals combine to form new and dangerous gases. Large cities without public transit systems and with unfavorable wind conditions suffer most. Thus, Los Angeles has a worse

Table 6–1 SOURCES AND TYPES OF AIR POLLUTION
(millions of tons annually, 1965)

	Carbon Monoxide	Sulfur Oxides	Nitrogen Oxides	Hydro-carbons	Particulate Matter	Totals
Motor vehicles	66	1	6	12	1	86
Industry	2	9	2	4	6	23
Powerplants	1	12	3	1	3	20
Space heating	2	3	1	1	1	8
Refuse disposal	1	1	1	1	1	5

Source: Joint Economic Committee, *The Economy, Energy and the Environment*, U.S. Congress, 1970.

[1] Joint Economic Committee, *The Economy, Energy and the Environment*, U.S. Congress, Washington, D. C. 1970.

air pollution problem than Chicago, although the two metropolitan areas have roughly equal populations. Los Angeles, with no rapid transit system, spreads over an area greater than that of Chicago. It burns 2,540 million gallons of gasoline daily, to 1,850 for Chicago. What is more, because of Chicago's wind, and California's frequent periods of stationary air, Los Angeles burned 231 gallons per cubic mile of air passing through the city, as against only 144 gallons for Chicago. Even in Chicago, or in cities with lower emission levels, air pollution is still a problem.[2]

Factory smoke, home heating, and garbage incineration add to auto exhausts to create pollution. These other sources can sometimes be controlled, as the cleanup of the air in Pittsburgh proved. Conversion from coal to natural gas, replacement of high sulfur fuel oil by higher grades from which sulfur is removed, controls over specific industrial processes, scrubbing of smoke, and use of garbage for landfills can reduce pollution. These substitutions are costly, and individual firms or citizens will not make them unless compelled by law or induced by tax mechanisms. Using sulfur free fuel for electric generation, for example, requires either that consumers pay higher rates or that electric companies' profits fall. Imposition of controls may be difficult, as when companies threaten to move or lay off workers if required to bear cleanup costs. However, if only a few sources of pollution are to blame, or if multiple sources (such as home incinerators) can easily be replaced by municipal services (such as garbage collection), control is easier than for automotive emissions.

Problems of Regulation

There are millions of automobile users. Most have no alternative to driving, at least some of the time. Regulating the amount of automotive travel is thus very difficult. Discussions of ways to induce drivers to switch to existing public transit systems show this. Replacement of automobile commuting by electrified mass transit would reduce emissions of hydrocarbons, carbon monoxide, lead, and nitrogen oxide. (Thermal electric generation may, however, cause some increase in sulfur oxide emission.) Economists have asked whether reducing fares or subsidizing free mass transit might tempt passengers to fill the trains. The estimates are not promising.

One study compared residents of Boston neighborhoods who face differing fares, riding times, and driving times to reach the central business district by subway and by automobile. It concluded that the number of trips to work made by public transit was not affected greatly by differences in fares. Cutting fares by half would increase transit use by less than 10 percent. Shopping trips are more responsive to fares. More people shop downtown when fares are lower, but this is not a shift from automobiles to subways. Use of public transit for commuting was more responsive to the relative times required to travel down-

[2] Panel of Technical Advisers on Automotive Air Pollution, *Report to the Joint State Government Commission, Pennsylvania,* 1963.

town by public and private modes of transit. Faster subways might lure a significant number of passengers away from their cars, but free transit alone would not.[3]

Another study compared commuting times by car and by elevated and commuter trains in Chicago. For most commuters, public modes took a longer time than driving. Evaluating each hour saved as worth an hour's wages to the commuter, the investigators found that for most commuters interviewed, it was cheaper to drive than to go by slower public transit systems. To make public modes equivalent in real cost, as long as they remained slower than roads, it would be necessary not only to make public transit free, but also to charge automobile users a dollar a day for entering the city.[4]

If public transit is fast and automobile use very expensive, commuters will use the trains. In New York, the subway is used for more than half of journeys to work. Public transit is used to a great extent in many European cities. But many commuters cannot be tempted, even by large subsidies, to switch from cars to public transit, because no public transit exists where they live and work. Although public transit may not be economical in small towns where few people travel between any two locations, there are still major cities, like Detroit and Los Angeles, that do not have rapid transit systems. Some parts of Los Angeles do not even have bus lines available to those who cannot drive. In other cities, public transit is often too slow to compete.

Economists often take this lack of rapid public transit as a given condition for their analyses and conclude, naturally, that driving cannot be eliminated. Even then, however, they may ask whether smaller, or cleaner, automobiles might reduce damage from pollution, and whether use of these less polluting cars could be induced by feasible controls or effluent charges.

Reducing of horsepower might be one alternative. A more powerful car uses more gasoline per mile than one with smaller engine capacity and produces more pollution when forced to drive below its high cruising speed on a crowded expressway. However, once consumers must buy automobiles anyway, many prefer cars that can carry their entire families on weekends and that they can also drive rapidly when they are not in town. A six cylinder compact car is the smallest that many find satisfactory. Comparison of demand for different automobiles at different price levels, and with different horsepower, has led one economist to argue that the price of an additional 1 percent of horsepower would have to rise more than 3 percent to induce a 1 percent reduction in power. Such small reductions would not have much effect on total emissions.[5] Fees for high-powered cars would have to be very great indeed to reduce pollution, and

[3] Gerald Kraft and Thomas Domencich, "Free Transit," in M. Edel and J. Rothenberg, *Readings in Urban Economics* (New York: Macmillan, 1972), pp. 459–80.

[4] L. N. Moses and H. F. Williamson, "Value of Time, Choice of Mode, and the Subsidy Issue in Urban Transportation," *Journal of Political Economy* (Vol. 71, No. 3, June 1963, pp. 247–64.

[5] Donald N. Dewees, "Costs and Effectiveness of Automobile Pollution Control Systems," unpublished paper, Harvard University, 1971.

such high fees would be resisted for the hardship they would bring to people who must drive between cities given the lack of good rail transport in the United States.

Studies do not indicate that raising the prices of all automobiles would reduce auto use greatly. Nor would an increase in gasoline taxes have much effect. Per mile gas costs are a small part of total motoring expenses. Past imposition of gasoline taxes has not reduced motoring noticeably in the United States, although considerably higher taxes in other countries may have had that effect. Given present transport systems and settlement patterns, it would take very severe bribes or charges to induce people not to use automobiles.

Fine tuning methods have also been suggested to make combustion in cars of present sizes somewhat cleaner. Taxes on lead in gasoline have been proposed. Standards for engine construction and exhaust controls are scheduled to become more stringent. These can reduce pollution somewhat, although at a cost of up to several hundred dollars for reconditioning used cars. But they are limited in their effect and will not end many air pollution problems. The nature of internal combustion gives the automotive designer a difficult choice. If combustion is incomplete, large amounts of carbon monoxide and hydrocarbons will be emitted. If combustion is made more efficient, or an afterburner is used, the generated heat leads to reactions that form nitrogen oxides. Most proposed pollution free cars merely improve combustion, thus increasing nitrogen oxide pollutants while reducing, but not eliminating, the others. If hydrocarbons or carbon monoxide alone were a problem, these devices could have great benefits. But nitrogen oxides also are a problem. Particularly when stagnant air is subjected to sunlight, as in a Los Angeles temperature inversion, hydrocarbons and nitrogen oxides react, producing nitrogen dioxide, oxidants, and a "photochemical smog." If the formation of these poisonous chemicals is limited by lack of nitrogen oxides, replacing some of the hydrocarbons and carbon monoxide in the air by nitrogen oxides may actually increase smog. Because none of the existing technologies can remove both hydrocarbons and nitrogen oxides completely, and because even a partial reduction is costly at existing horsepower levels, economists sometimes have doubted whether much net benefit improvement in the air will be possible from controls.[6]

The Wrong Conclusion

It is sometimes concluded from this that nothing can be done to eliminate automotive air pollution. The consumer is said to have chosen the automobile consciously, and, in the process, to have accepted pollution as the price of keeping a big, fast, private car. Psychological theories have even been developed to explain this choice. They claim that the American—particularly the male American—is irrationally attached to his car. The automobile represents power, compensates for deep-seated fears of impotence, or allows avoidance of personal

[6] Paul B. Downing and Lytton W. Stoddard, "The Economics of Air Pollution Control for Used Cars," unpublished paper, University of California, Riverside, 1971.

contact with other commuters. Among some people it is fashionable to consider their fellows as half-insane for driving.

Many people do enjoy driving, although most prefer it when roads are not crowded. Undoubtedly, some people do have their self-esteem lifted by ownership of a fancy car. However, in Manhattan, where automotive commuting is prohibitively expensive, people rent cars for pleasure outings, take subways to work, and find other ways to keep up with the Joneses. Psychological manipulation may help auto companies sell new model cars more often, but there is no need to assume the consumer is irrational, to explain his driving. The lack of alternatives is sufficient explanation. If one must work to eat, and must drive to get to work, then one must drive to eat. Even a person who hates driving cannot change highway patterns through individual actions, and most have to commute by car. In the language of economics, this is *rational suboptimizing* or making the best of a bad situation.

The relation of each driver to others can be described by what game theorists call the *prisoner's dilemma*, after the case of two suspects, each of whom is told separately by the district attorney that the other is likely to confess to a crime. Confession will bring a light sentence, but if both remain quiet, they will go free. Because each must fear that the other will confess, in which case his sentence may be harsh, each will confess to keep his risk small. In any prisoner's dilemma situation, one course can yield everyone the best result if everyone follows it. But if not everyone follows it, then those who do make the attempt suffer a great loss. Unless there is some mechanism for ensuring that others will make the attempt, it is therefore rational to accept a suboptimal outcome and not try for the best possible result. This is the case with the automobile. For each individual it may be irrational not to drive, unless enough others also stop driving and demand good public transit.

In this situation, to seek a psychological explanation for why individuals drive is to ask the wrong question. The problem is not why individuals drive, given the options open to them. It is why the options in American cities involve few alternatives to life in residential neighborhoods that require automobiles be used for work, shopping, and other necessary activities.

Asking why the options are limited involves questions that go beyond estimating the costs and benefits of using any one automobile. It involves asking why cities are so big in the first place.[7] It involves asking why more research is not directed to producing alternatives to the internal combustion engine.[8] It involves asking, too, why cities take the form they now have; why there is not more public investment in rapid transit systems; and why internal combustion, on the other hand, does receive so much government support.

---

[7] The total population is not the answer because 85 percent of the U.S. inhabitants live on less than 2 percent of the land. The growth of big business, concentrating productive assets into fewer and fewer organizations, may be part of the answer because it draws people to cities where major factories and headquarters are located (see Chapter 7). A full answer remains to be discovered.

[8] As long as the automobile is a necessity, auto companies know it cannot be banned, and so have little incentive to look for alternatives. They are well off now. Those interested in transport research, however, can often get little funding elsewhere.

Ignoring these questions of why options are limited leads to the wrong conclusion about the sources of pollution. To blame the psychological problems of the individual who drives is "blaming the victim" of the problem.[9] To tax driving may be "penalizing the victim." An effluent charge might be more of a burden to low income commuters than to the wealthy. Because most workers in American cities (except New York) drive to work, a fee for commuting that costs each family the same amount of money would take a larger percentage of the earnings of low wage workers than of incomes of the more affluent. This is what is called a *regressive* tax. A tax geared to exact production of effluents might be even more regressive, because poorer commuters buy used cars that allow more pollutants to escape into the atmosphere. Such regressive taxes are not only considered socially undesirable by many economists; they would also be opposed by the majority of working commuters. Civil rights organizations and labor unions have complained that attacks on the automobile would place a burden on the poor, and that a commuter tax in the name of ecology might amount to taxing the poor to subsidize playgrounds for the rich. Even businesses which would not pay the taxes might oppose them because if workers could not drive to jobs, this would cause the businesses problems when they tried to hire workers.

URBAN SETTLEMENT AND TRANSPORT

Commuting first became a problem when cities grew after the industrial revolution. The growth of large factories, and of commercial districts from which the factories were managed, led to the concentration of many people into cities. The separation of residential and business areas became possible because of several interrelated inventions: the trolley car, the subway, and the automobile, on the one hand; the elevator and the skyscraper, on the other. More offices could crowd into business districts than was possible in walk-up buildings, more people could live within commuting range than was possible when only walking and horsedrawn vehicles could be used. However, inventions did not make urban sprawl and a dependence on the automobile inevitable. They only made it possible. Institutional reasons must be found for why the fearsome possibility was realized.

Why Suburbs Sprawl

Even in large cities, compact settlement patterns might reduce automobile commuting, and people might live closer to business districts or in nodes close to rapid transit stations. This would require that more multifamily dwellings be

[9] William Ryan, *Blaming the Victim* (New York: Random House, 1971), shows a number of cases in which people are blamed for their own misfortune. Many of these involve misapplication of natural science, as well as economics, as when Darwinian theories of evolution or heredity are misapplied to claim that anyone who does not succeed is necessarily "unfit," rather than considering the structure of the economy.

built. Families may prefer to live in single family homes than to live in apartments, at least if the price differential is not too great. However, they might
accept change if they had to pay the full cost the present commuting pattern
imposes on society, and if an alternative were really available. At present, however, alternatives are limited, and incentives reward, rather than charge, families
for living in suburbs and driving to work. These are institutional biases in the
organization of the urban economy. Society could change them, but the individual commuter cannot.

The theory of externalities explains one reason for urban sprawl. A service
will be overused if each user, when making decisions, does not take into account the costs he imposed on other users. Highway use creates several external
diseconomies. In congested traffic, each driver slows down the other users of a
road. The more cars that try to cover a stretch of road every minute, the fewer
that may actually drive the entire distance in that time. Each commuter who
buys a house at the end of a freeway takes congestion as given and does not
consider what his presence will do to other drivers. When many commuters do
this, all find they are slowed down. A commuter highway, in this sense, is like a
common pasture or fishery. If not regulated, it will be overused.[10]

Commuters also impose external costs on those not using freeways. As
cars drive downtown from suburbs, they pass other neighborhoods. New highways disrupt communities by taking land from some facilities and homes and
leaving those that remain with fewer neighbors to support local services. Once in
use, highways are a source of noise and air pollution.[11] There is little wonder
that in neighborhoods through which highways are to be built, residents often
oppose construction.

These external costs, imposed by commuters on less suburban neighborhoods, are not reflected in the costs of commuting. The costs are hard to measure, and highway departments, which are supposed to compensate those dispos-
sessed by construction, often fail to measure them. The costs thus give no
disincentive to buying a home in the suburbs and driving to work. Rather, they
are an incentive to people in the inner rings of a city to move further to the
suburbs. By suburbanizing, they can escape these costs for which they will not
be compensated by the drivers. External diseconomies without compensation
thus are a cause for greater urban sprawl.

Externalities, as Chapter 4 showed, only distort incentives because of the
specific institutions of an economy. Economists and highway engineers could set
tolls that would charge road users for the congestion they impose on other
drivers and for damage to neighborhoods disrupted by commuter roads. These
institutions are not introduced. Suburban housing developers know they can only

---

[10] A. A. Walters, "The Theory and Measurement of Private and Social Costs of Highway Congestion," in Edel and Rothenberg, op. cit., pp. 417–39.
[11] A report of the California Department of Public Health, *Lead in the Environment and Its
Effects on Humans*, showed persons living far from freeways had 16 micrograms of lead for each 100
grams of blood; those living near freeways had 22.7 micrograms. Traffic police had higher concentrations.

sell homes if good, toll-free roads are built. They can be counted on to lobby for roads. Those already living in suburbs, who have bought homes at high prices and have mortgages to pay off, also resist tolls. In the past, residents of the generally poorer neighborhoods closer to the centers of cities were not organized enough to meet this pressure. If they can achieve more power and demand compensation or block new construction, it would be a case in which equality improved the efficiency of resource use. Up to now, however, the pro-highway forces have generally been stronger, and damages remain uncompensated.

A number of other institutions also reward those who move to the suburbs. One is the division of metropolitan areas into separate towns with distinct tax bases. Central city governments often must provide services used by the entire metropolitan area, as well as special services to poor people who live in the older neighborhoods. Those who live in suburbs often avoid the property taxes that support these services. Even when per capita government costs are equal in all neighborhoods, a wealthier community can keep its tax down to a smaller percentage rate on residents' wealth by becoming a separate town. When state laws allow suburbs to remain independent jurisdictions, as they do for most American metropolitan areas, the result is the separation of low-tax suburbs from high-tax central cities and inner ring towns. This in turn leads to a vicious circle of oversuburbanization. The wealthiest people left in the city at each round flee to the suburbs to reduce their tax burdens. Those left behind must either reduce the quality of public services or raise taxes. Either response leads to new incentives to suburbanization.

Another institution with similar effects is the availability of easier credit on some purchases than for others. Government supported mortgage credit to suburban homeownership, combined with private credit for auto loans, encourages ownership of homes and automobiles rather than other consumer goods and services on which money might be spent by a person who chooses apartment life and a shorter commuting radius. The United States tax system also subsidizes private homes by allowing the deduction of interest and property tax payments. Subsidies on rental properties are less easily obtained and may not give rent reductions to the actual residents. Condominium arrangements allow apartments in high rise dwellings to receive single family tax treatment but are complicated to arrange. Real estate assessments are sometimes more lenient for single family dwellings than for rental apartment buildings; and the general property tax, by taxing buildings rather than just land, reduces tax costs for speculative holding of idle land. This speculation may force builders of new dwellings to choose sites farther from the central city.

Problems of Public Transit

120

These institutional biases and externalities give a strong incentive to American families to live in the suburbs. However, even with this settlement pattern, it might be possible to develop public transport systems. These systems would not be as efficient as those that would be possible given more concentrated settlement patterns. However, if they were provided, and roads for the commuters were not built as readily as they are now, suburbanites might reduce auto use.

In most American cities, this is not even attempted. Roads for commuters are built regularly; rapid transit systems are rarely constructed, and most of those in use are financial failures. From a peak of 23 billion rides per year at the end of World War II, total public transit use, including subways, trolleys, buses, and commuter trains declined to 8 billion by 1967. Subway rides fell less drastically, from 2.7 billion to 1.9 billion. The high wartime figures may have been inflated because cars were unavailable and gasoline rationed, but the decline continued long after the emergency controls ended.

Why did use of public transit decline? In part, a movement of people from older neighborhoods served by transit systems to new suburbs reduced ridership. But this is not a full explanation. Subways were not built to follow the riders. Bus lines only partially replaced the trolley lines that were torn up. Use of remaining lines declined and complaints about fares and services increased. This occurred for several reasons.

One problem is a need for subsidy that stems from the difficulties of running an enterprise on a break-even basis in the presence of economies of scale. That additional customers can use a service with little cost to the system ought to be an advantage to the public. But it also involves problems familiar to economists. If a subway has empty seats, if new cars can be added to an existing train, or if trains can run more often on existing tracks, the marginal cost of adding passengers will be low. If the benefit of carrying an additional passenger covers marginal cost, the economist argues the passenger should be induced to ride the train. The principle that operation should expand until marginal cost equals marginal benefit is the same one used in evaluating pollution control in Chapter 5. It can be presumed that marginal benefit is at least as great as what an added passenger would be willing to pay. Thus, if it costs five cents per additional passenger to double the number of riders on a subway system, and a nickel fare would lead to a doubling compared to the number riding with existing twenty-five cent fares, economists would approve the fare reduction. Even zero fare would be considered optimal if it were needed to fill the larger train, and if each passenger added reduced air pollution more than five cents worth by not using his car.

To break even, however, subways must not only pay the marginal costs of transporting extra passengers. They also must bear the fixed costs of maintaining their facilities and paying off the debts incurred for their original construction. These costs are particularly high because capacity must be great enough to handle rush hour crowds. If these fixed total costs are divided by the number of passengers on a system, the resulting fixed cost per rider must be added to the average operating cost per rider to compute the average cost per rider of the system. This average cost will be greater than the marginal cost added by an addi-

121

tional rider. If the fare, which is paid by all riders, is to attract enough riders to equalize marginal costs and benefits, it will be less than average cost. Thus, on every rider, the average revenue collected will be less than the average cost. If the line attracts the optimal number of passengers, it will suffer a loss, as shown in Fig. 6–1.

To the economist, this is a normal and justifiable loss. The transit line should receive a subsidy so it can cover costs without driving away riders through high fares. The governments that have control over public transit have not seen it that way. They demand that transit systems break even, an institu-

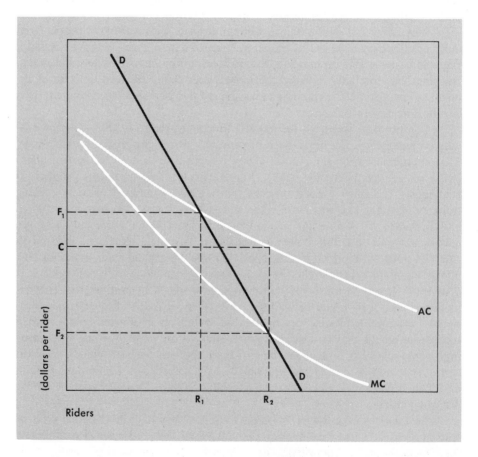

FIG. 6–1 The need for transit subsidy. *DD* is the demand curve for a transit mode. *AC* and *MC* are the average and marginal costs. With more riders, these costs fall because of more complete use of large scale capacity. If a fare of F_1 is set, revenues of F_2 per rider will cover costs averaging F_1 per rider. The system will break even. A fare of F_1 is efficient because it will attract all riders willing to pay their marginal cost. However, at this fare, the average cost per rider is C, and a deficit of $C - F_2$ per rider occurs. A subsidy of (R_2) × ($C - F_2$) is required.

tional requirement that forces lines to raise their fares and drive away riders. Sometimes they have also saddled public transit systems, acquired from private owners, with heavy debt burdens. The private owners sold to the government because lines couldn't operate profitably, so that one might think that the government could have bought the lines cheaply. Often, however, cities borrowed money to pay high prices for the money-losing lines. Thereafter, the transit systems were burdened with annual fixed costs for interest payments that made the need for subsidy greater.

The result has been, for some subway systems, a spiral of increasing fares, decreased ridership, and growing deficits. High fares, however, are not the only problem. Poor facilities are even more serious. Declining numbers of passengers and rising deficits led city governments to think that new investments in subways and other transit facilities would prove unjustified. This was not necessarily a correct conclusion. The studies that show low or zero fares might not attract riders also show that faster or more frequent trains, by reducing trip times, might make a difference.[12] More comfortable trains, not considered in the studies, might make a difference. But cities did not spend the money for these improvements or even, in some cases, the money needed to subsidize adequate repair of their equipment. In the United States, no well-designed, well-operated and adequately subsidized public transit system has ever really been given the chance to attract riders.

The Subsidized Highways

The need for subsidies is no less for highways than for public transit. To cover the cost of highway building, maintenance, and policing, funds must be collected. However, if tolls are charged on uncongested roads to cover average costs, ridership might be discouraged excessively. Not surprisingly, tolls are almost never collected on rural roads and streets within residential districts. Even commuter routes, for which tolls are sometimes charged, have generally received subsidies in the United States. When suburbs build roads, inner cities are forced to expand facilities because of rising congestion levels. Repair, policing, and environmental costs are all borne by local communities or by the states, out of general tax revenues. For construction itself, there is also an abundant source of cheap money. This construction receives all of the proceeds of a national tax on gasoline. These funds are deposited in a Highway Trust Fund, and distributed to the states for construction of the Interstate Highway System. The states must pay only 10 percent of construction costs—through their own gasoline taxes. Between 1956, when it was created, and 1970, $40 billion had been invested in the Interstate Highway System.

---

[12] These studies might suggest fare increases were not a problem at all. Historically, however, fare increases may have had an effect that could not now be reversed by decreases. As fares rose, people bought cars or moved away from transit lines. Once they had done so, lower fares could no longer attract them back, although increasing fares could drive still more riders away.

Financing highway construction out of a gasoline tax that is uniform throughout the country involves a large subsidy to urban highways. In cities, automobiles drive fewer miles to the gallon, than in rural areas; more automobiles also use each mile of road. So, gasoline revenues for each mile of road are greater than in the country. However, the construction cost of each mile of road is also much higher. More overpasses or underpasses for connecting streets are required, as are more entrances and exits. Land acquisition, demolition of buildings, and compensation of former landowners are also more expensive (although the highway system pays inadequate compensation). Construction costs in a city will often be 5 to 10 million dollars per mile for a six-lane highway, although rural costs are often under one million dollars.[13] Travelers driving between cities or in some rural areas thus subsidize the highways for urban commuters. Of course, the intercity drivers themselves are often forced to drive and to pay the gas tax subsidy to urban highways because of institutions that have made good passenger trains for journeys of up to several hundred miles unavailable in the United States, although they operate effectively in Europe.[14]

The subsidization of highways is not the only benefit the automobile commuter receives. The oil depletion allowance, which allows producers of petroleum substantial tax savings, may reduce gasoline prices to the driver. Faced with heavily subsidized automotive commuting and with low-quality public transit that the government has generally refused to subsidize adequately, it is not surprising that most commuters take to the roads. This choice is not the result of psychological idiosyncrasies, but rather of the alternatives available. These alternatives, in turn, are the result of political decisions to subsidize highways much more than other modes of ground transport. At one level, the Highway Trust Fund appears to be the travelers' choice—the Congress and the state governments that allow it to continue are elected by the public, including the many travelers. Governmental officials, however, are not elected on the issue of highways alone. People select candidates for positions on foreign policy, wages and employment, or other issues. Elected officials and the voters themselves may also be limited by institutions from finding alternative transit systems to support.

THE POLITICAL ECONOMY OF LIMITED ALTERNATIVES

The lack of alternatives to driving is, in some people's view, sustained by the political power of economic interests. The *highway lobby* of beneficiaries has been compared in power to the "military-industrial complex." An array of well-financed organizations argue for more highways at every session of Congress. The American Road Builders' Association, representing highway engi-

[13] J. R. Meyer, J. F. Kain, and M. Wohl, *The Urban Transportation Problem* (Cambridge: Harvard University Press, 1966), p. 205.

[14] Theodore Keeler, "The Economics of Passenger Trains," *Journal of Business*, Vol. 44, No. 2, April 1971, pp. 148–74.

neering and construction material companies; the Associated General Contractors of America; the National Highway Users Conference, representing trucking and bus companies, among other users; American Trucking Associations, Inc.; and numerous organizations of the asphalt, concrete, petroleum, rubber, and other industries are always on hand. An American Association of State Highway Officials represents agencies whose organizational growth depends on federal highway funds. The American Automobile Association, which enrolls members by offering towing and trip-planning services, devotes a large proportion of its funds to similar lobbying.[15] The political pressure activities of the automobile companies themselves have received more publicity through their constant battles with Ralph Nader in recent years.

These organizations are clearly able to command more resources and mobilize them more quickly than the residents of neighborhoods threatened by highways, or the half of all Americans shown by public opinion polls to prefer autos only because other modes of transport are not adequately available. This is not to say that the highway lobby is invincible. The Lower Manhattan Expressway, the Boston Inner Belt, and some other routes have been blocked by public opposition. Some subsidies for mass transit and limited safety and pollution controls have been passed by state and federal legislatures. However, these defeats came too late to prevent a proliferation of urban freeways, and enforcement of environmental controls remains uncertain.

To mention a lobby is not, however, to explain a political process. The explanation that transport options are limited because of big business power is often presented in fallacious terms. The problem of "monopolies" is often referred to when monopolistic price behavior itself is not the problem. Even the size and wealth of companies, which certainly allows large businesses to exert political pressure, does not explain why there are no sources of *countervailing power* to balance the pressure of economic interests. The political explanation of limited alternatives requires an explanation of this lack of counterpressure, as well as a demonstration of who favors highways.

One important example of pressures and lack of counterpressure is the petroleum industry. The industry's power has been discussed since the muckrakers attacked John D. Rockefeller at the turn of the century. Although the Supreme Court ordered the breakup of Rockefeller's original Standard Oil Company, the industry still is the preserve of very large companies. Fifteen of the sixty largest American corporations in 1968 were petroleum producers. Four former branches of the original Standard Oil—Standard Oil of New Jersey (Esso and Humble), Mobil (formerly Standard Oil of New York), Standard Oil of California (Chevron), and Standard Oil of Indiana (Amoco)—as well as Texaco, Gulf, and the American branch of Shell were among the twenty-five largest firms. British Petroleum and Shell Company were among the twenty-five largest firms based outside the United States. Oil was the basis of some of the largest private

125

---

15 Helen Leavitt, *Superhighway Superhoax* (Garden City: Doubleday, 1970), pp. 107–50.

fortunes of the century, from Rockefeller's in refining to Getty's in production, Hughes's in drilling tools, and Onassis's in tankship operation. Petroleum industries have been controversial not only because of the role of the automobile but also because of their involvement in foreign policy, and because of recent ecological problems caused by transport and production of oil. Highways, lax enforcement of environmental protection, and even foreign coups all seem to benefit the petroleum companies. But what is the basis of their power?

Is Monopoly the Problem?

One commonly held view is that the problem is simply *monopoly* in the petroleum industry. This is too facile, at least insofar as environmental problems are concerned. The most common aspect of monopoly is an ability to raise prices by limiting production, because competitors are few or nonexistent. In this sense, it is not certain whether the petroleum industry is presently a monopoly. What is more, reduced production and higher prices for petroleum products would not be an environmental problem. A fine tuning advocate might even suggest they could help cure the problem.

Before the First World War, petroleum was a monopoly in the United States and a duopoly on the world market. Standard Oil and a European consortium were the only significant producers. Later, seven large companies shared control of the world market. Until the late 1950s, these companies could fix prices as a monopoly would. More recently, however, the industry has become more competitive. New private producers and government owned companies in several countries have entered the world market. The biggest companies retain enough of the distribution and refining facilities to exercise a strong influence on price, but they can no longer rule at will. Expanded production led to one round of price cutting in the late 1950s. Companies must be concerned about the costs of oil production because they are faced with international competitors.

This competition creates several environmental problems. If prices have any effect on automobile use, price cutting leads to increased internal combustion and hence to more pollution. The monopolistic competition of an increased number of companies also requires each company to maintain its own gasoline stations. Often there will be several service stations at one intersection. Bringing oil to each station from the refinery of its brand, rather than the nearest refinery, increases transportation costs. Finally, there is increased environmental damage in production.

When the East Texas oil field was discovered in 1930, thousands of "wildcat" operators began drilling. An oil field is a common resource. The different wells all draw from the same deposit of petroleum. Each one can reduce production in other wells both by taking oil and by reducing gas pressure in the underground "dome." Reduced pressure makes it more costly to pump petroleum out and leaves some impossible to extract. When many drillers rush to beat their competitors to the oil, total production is reduced; and natural gas, which, if captured, is a cleaner fuel than gasoline, may also be wasted.

126

As in other cases of common resources, there was an economic argument for conservation legislation. New laws, however, were not prompted by ecological considerations. Rather, wildcat oil depressed prices and allowed small refineries to compete with the major oil companies. The companies demanded protection from competition. The Texas Railroad Commission was given the power to limit overdrilling, but only in a particular manner. Minimum distances between wells were imposed, but they were smaller than the distances that an efficiently planned oilfield would have used. The principal regulation was *prorationing*, a limit to the number of days a month each well could operate. This system left inefficient or wasteful wells operating as much of the time as wells with better conservation practices. It did not remove the incentive to drill more wells to increase one's share of the total oil take. Because it did limit production, the price was stabilized, especially after a federal Hot Oil Act prohibited interstate transport of oil not approved by the states. Independent refiners were forced to come to terms with the big companies for supplies. For the oil industry, this was conservation enough.

International competition of big companies created similar problems in the 1960s. Although the companies might regulate production among themselves most of the time to keep prices stable, their oligopoly was fragile. Each feared others might find a source of oil much cheaper by far than those of other producers and undercut their prices. This led to increased exploration and a scramble for drilling rights in countries throughout the world. Production costs are often lower on new oil fields, where gas pressure is highest. Companies began drilling in new areas, seeking immediate cost advantages and protection against being undersold. One result was drilling from fields before natural gas pipelines could be installed. The gas itself, a cleaner fuel than oil, was wasted. Undersea oil fields were tapped before safe technologies in this extraction could be developed. Arctic oil fields were opened, requiring the laying of pipe lines in cold climates, and fields far from markets were exploited requiring transport in giant "supertankers." Oil slicks and possible damage to arctic ecosystems were risked in the rush to produce at low cost. The companies claimed these risks were required to prevent a shortage of oil. In fact, older high-cost fields still had large reserves of oil that could meet demand adequately for many years while safer technologies for tapping new sources were developed. Oil companies, however, raced to open new fields ahead of competition, knowing they would not have to bear many of the environmental costs anyway. Compared to this competition, monopoly hardly seems a greater threat to the environment.

Petroleum and Political Power

Monopolies or not, petroleum companies have great size and economic strength. The major oil producers all command large sums of money for influencing voters' and legislators' opinions. Even independent drilling operators are often wealthy enough to play prominent political roles through their campaign contributions. The direct political involvement of the oil companies was perhaps

127

most apparent in the debate over the so-called Tidelands Oil bill. This act was designed to allow states to grant leases for undersea oil fields under the continental shelf up to three miles out to sea. The oil fields had previously belonged to the federal government. The lobbying effort to secure passage of the bill became famous in its intensity. Even the name of the bill was the creation of the oil companies' press agent. The true *tidelands* are those shores covered by water at high tide, but not at low tide. These lands have always been under state jurisdiction. Calling the continental shelf "tidelands" was designed to make people think it ought to belong to the states. Congress twice passed the bill, only to have it vetoed by President Truman. Contributions by oil magnates not only to the 1952 Republican presidential campaign but also to the 1948 Dixiecrat ticket, which split the Democratic vote, have been attributed to the Tidelands issue. The Secretary of the Interior claimed that $300,000 had been offered to the Democratic campaign fund earlier if the Department of Justice would drop the Federal claim. Finally, in 1953, the Submerged Lands Act, giving the rights to the states, was passed and signed.[16]

Federal support of highway building, CIA involvements in countries that have challenged petroleum companies, and a pattern of subsidies to oil production have been cited as evidence of an "empire of oil." Some of these privileges increase gasoline usage. The oil depletion allowance permits producers to deduct from profits an amount equal to 22½ percent of the value of crude oil produced (before 1970 it was 27½ percent) before computing taxes. This almost exempts crude oil producers from taxes. It is called an equivalent to depreciation allowances on industrial investments, but depreciation on the actual oil rigs is permitted, too, and costs of drilling dry wells are written off as business expenses. Overseas drilling is also rewarded by provisions that foreign tax payments can be counted as credits against United States taxes. Calling rents to foreign governments "taxes" can allow an additional reduction in U.S. tax payments. Finally, apart from gasoline taxes for highway building, other taxes on petroleum are avoided.

All of this support can lead to expanded investment in petroleum production. The limits to production imposed by prorationing and quotas on imported oil only partially offset this expansion. In part because of lower taxes, and in part because of subsidies, per gallon gasoline prices to the consumer are lower in the United States than in most countries. Although fine tuning automobile demand by additional taxes on gasoline might not have any immediate effect on consumption, the long history of subsidized gasoline may have encouraged the original spread of suburbs.

Critics of the oil industry, since the days of John D. Rockefeller, have cited special benefits to the industry, or specific political protection of the companies' interests. What, however, do these reports prove? Does benefit from a government policy prove undue influence? Reports of lobbying and other pres-

16 Harvey O'Connor, *The Empire of Oil* (New York: Monthly Review Press, 1962).

sures are often unconfirmed; even those that are public knowledge are hard to evaluate. It is often argued that interest-group activity is a normal and justifiable method of influencing policy in a democracy, as long as other interests have their chance to present their case and wield countervailing power.[17] To argue that the petroleum companies (or others in the highway lobby) are part of an institutional pattern that causes overuse of the automobile and environmental damage, it is necessary to argue why the development of countervailing power faces systematic obstacles.

Obstacles to Countervailing Power

Many groups in the economy could benefit from limitations to highway building and reduced benefits to petroleum companies. Environmental organizations and consumer groups sometimes attempt to organize against the lobbying efforts of oil companies and highway lobbies. Certainly, most taxpayers could benefit from the removal of oil depletion loopholes. Communities threatened by pollution, state governments that are unable to collect much in taxes from oil companies, and proponents of investments (including subways) that compete with highways for funds all have a stake in the development of an antipetroleum pressure group. However, such a coalition rarely develops any strength.

Why is this so? One simple argument invokes the notion that legislation itself is a public good, of the sort discussed in Chapter 5. If laws are passed that limit or tax petroleum companies, many people will benefit, whether they have worked for these laws or not. Working for change, however, involves spending time and money, and perhaps taking personal risks. When a large number of people each have only a little to gain, it is argued, these costs and risks create a prisoner's dilemma situation. Nobody will take the first steps to organization, although all would benefit if everybody did.[18] (On the other hand, the few oil companies more easily can coordinate their actions and share the costs of lobbying from which they benefit.)

This argument is suggestive, but not conclusive. After all, some organizations have been formed that bring together large numbers of people for political purposes. If the prisoner's dilemma is viewed too rigidly, it is hard to explain how labor unions ever came to be, given the risks organizers faced.[19] One must ask, also, in the case of the lack of opposition to the petroleum and highway lobbies, why the costs or risks of organization are so high, compared to possibilities of coordinating action to overcome the risks, that the interested public does not act.

The answer seems to be that the workings of the economic system make

[17] John Kenneth Galbraith, *American Capitalism: The Concept of Countervailing Power* (Boston: Houghton Mifflin, 1952).

[18] Mancur Olson, Jr., *The Logic of Collective Action* (Cambridge: Harvard University Press, 1965).

[19] Barry Weisberg, "Raping Alaska: The Ecology of Oil" in Editors of Ramparts, *Eco-Catastrophe* (San Francisco: Canfield Press, 1970), pp. 106–28.

many people dependent, in the short run, on the successful operation of oil companies and highways, although in the long run they could benefit from change. This takes place at several levels in society. Locally, voters approve highway expenditures because they have no alternative means of access to jobs, shopping, and recreation, given the existence of a Highway Trust Fund but no equally generous subsidies for rail transport. The communities that will be threatened by roads are more easily organized against construction because the benefits of keeping their homes make the risks of organizing worth bearing. This often leads to conflict between the drivers who need the roads and the communities that oppose them. The conflict makes it harder for both groups to realize, and organize around, a possible common interest in building rapid transit systems instead of roads.

A similar phenomenon operates when conservation measures are discussed. Workers and small businessmen may depend on the jobs and business of oil companies for a livelihood. Because America does not guarantee workers jobs in their own communities, people must be concerned that investment take place near where they live. Businesses also depend on the cheapness of fuel for their operation. Thus, when conservationists in Maine opposed the opening of a refinery for environmental reasons, manufacturers who needed cheap oil to compete and workers who needed jobs supported the refinery. The possible common interests of conservationists and workers or oil consumers in national conservation and fuel policies are ignored as they fight over short-run issues.

Similarly, the oil companies can play states off against each other. This is why they were so interested in giving the states, rather than the federal government, the rights to lease "tidelands" oil. The advantages of dealing with states were apparent after the Alaska oil strike in 1969. Alaska auctioned off leases to the Prudhoe Bay fields for $900 million. This sum is small compared to the federal budget. The oil companies save approximately as much in taxes every two years because of depletion allowances. The sums may also have seemed low to the companies; it has been suggested that a less hasty sale might have drawn higher prices. For a state government, however, it is a very large sum. Development also promised the state a 12.5 percent royalty and a 4 percent severance tax on the oil produced. Alaska therefore hastened to lease the land, and the oil companies could rush to develop it without any requirement of a delay to develop safety measures for drilling and transport of oil in tundra conditions.

Even at the national level, the petroleum companies have the advantage of divided opponents. They can pressure nations with threats to invest elsewhere or allow industrial fuel prices to rise, if they are not protected from taxes or controls. The next chapter argues why rivalry over growth is built in to the structure of capitalist and some planned economies. This makes these countries unable to place too many controls on the biggest investors.

For this reason, even the federal government is no great threat to oil company actions. Ironically, despite the tidelands lobbying effort, the infamous

Santa Barbara Channel oil spill occurred on a drilling platform outside of the state-controlled areas. Local leaders in Santa Barbara, which is a wealthy community, had enough influence that California did not allow drilling on its part of the shelf close to the city. But outside the three mile limit, the federal government issued a lease in 1968, without asking the local government for its opinions. The next January, a well sprung a leak, filling the channel with oil and destroying beaches and wildlife. Despite the efforts of local citizens and nationwide attention to the disaster, the Federal Government only ordered drilling to stop for a brief period of time, and then allowed it to continue on the claim that removing all of the oil from beneath the channel would be the only way to ensure safety. This, however, was estimated to be a job requiring more than ten years. The oil company involved was, in short, allowed to go ahead with business as usual. Although it might face eventual court claims for damages to private property, these were apparently not a sufficient deterrent to further drilling. The ruling was made on the basis of scientific data provided by the companies, which was kept secret by the government so as to protect the private rights of the companies, even when conservation groups demanded that their scientists have the right to examine and contest the companies' claims. The California Attorney General himself commented that the companies were "preventing oil drilling experts from aiding the Attorney General's office in its lawsuits over the Santa Barbara oil spill."

SUMMARY

Petroleum combustion by automobiles in urban areas is one of the principal sources of air pollution. Economic analysis shows that it is not a source that could be reduced easily by fine tuning of incentives to the individual driver. This chapter surveyed a number of institutional factors which increase automobile commuting and petroleum use. These include subsidies and externalities that give urban residents an incentive to live in suburbs and commute by car, and public policies that favor the automobile and petroleum industries and oppose mass public transit. Transport technologies were a necessary factor in this development, and the power of petroleum companies and the highway lobby exert pressure against change. Underlying all these forces, however, are a number of vicious circles in the organization of society that make change more difficult.

The prisoner's dilemma concept of game theory was used to analyze these vicious circles. This concept describes cases in which one course of action is preferable for many people, if they all attempt that course. However, it is unlikely to succeed for one individual alone. Remaining in central cities and securing good public transit are options often prevented by the prisoner's dilemma.

There are strong incentives leading people to flee the cities for the suburbs; equally strong incentives lead them to drive. Effluent charges, or other means to

131

make automobile use more costly, would leave them worse off, because alternatives to driving remain undeveloped. So, they do not support local environmental controls and avoid the existing subways. If, however, enough people used the subways or remained in town instead of fleeing to suburbs, cities and mass transit systems could be improved.

Similarly, at the local, state, or national level, prisoner's dilemmas created by economic institutions divide the opponents of petroleum companies and automotive commuting. These opponents come into conflict over short-run issues of tax revenue, growth, jobs, and accessibility. They find it hard to take the risks and bear the cost of organizing that could create new institutions to alter the terms under which jobs, energy, and transportation are available.

The result is that 86 million tons of pollutants are emitted by cars, and thus the economist must agree that, given present institutions, the benefits of effluent taxes or other fine tuning might outweigh the costs. This, however, is a result of the existence of a two-level prisoner's dilemma situation. Neither as driving consumer, nor as voter, has the citizen really shown he "prefers" the automobile and the public support of oil and other companies, as psychological theories argue. Rather, the organization of the economy has made the costs of options or organization appear too high to each citizen, although to everyone (except oil and auto companies) it is really suboptimal.

General accounts of energy use and automotive pollution include Panel on Electrically Powered Vehicles, *The Automobile and Air Pollution* (Washington: Department of Commerce, 1967); Joint Economic Committee, *The Economy, Energy and the Environment* (Washington: U.S. Government Printing Office, 1970); and Resources for the Future, *U.S. Energy Policies: An Agenda for Research* (Baltimore: John Hopkins Press, 1968). The economic problems of commuting and urban land use are explored in *Readings in Urban Economics*, Matthew Edel and Jerome Rothenberg, eds. (New York: Macmillan, 1968), and in K. N. Schaefer and E. Sclar, *Access* (Baltimore: Penguin Books (In Press). A longer perspective is presented in Lewis Mumford, *The City in History* (New York: Harcourt, Brace and World, 1961). A popular account of the highway program is Helen Leavitt, *Superhighway-Superhoax* (Garden City: Doubleday, 1970). On the petroleum industry, see Edith T. Penrose, *The Large International Firm in Developing Countries* (Cambridge, Mass.: M.I.T. Press, 1968); M. A. Adelman, P. G. Bradley, and C. A. Norman, *Alaskan Oil* (New York: Praeger, 1971); Harvey O'Connor, *World Crisis in Oil* (New York: Monthly Review Press, 1962); and Robert Engler, *The Politics of Oil* (New York: Macmillan, 1961). Similar analyses of other industries and their environmental effects appear in the various "Nader Reports."

Economic Systems:

Growth or Change?

CHAPTER SEVEN

Economic growth has been associated with increasing pollution. The last three chapters showed how depletion and overuse of material and waste dispersal resources occurred as industrial and economic growth accelerated. Institutional reasons for some environmental damage were cited. Producers and consumers pollute when systems of property rights leave social costs external to decision maker's rewards. Decision makers may be given no alternatives to pollution because of prisoner's dilemma situations. Improved design of economic systems could allow some growth with less pollution than in the past.

This does not mean *unlimited* growth can be pollution free. At some point, energy use requirements for recycling other resources would be prohibitive. The world is not necessarily near this limit yet. If better energy sources, such as clean thermonuclear fusion, can be developed, considerable growth will be possible. However, some writers react to present problems and to the eventual limits to growth by proclaiming an immediate need to stop all world economic growth. Chapters 2 and 3 suggest this is not desirable. Many countries require further growth to reach standards of adequate nutrition and income at which population growth would be expected to slow. Even if zero population growth were possible, stopping industrialization in the less-developed countries would perpetuate severe inequalities in world income. Even those who do not consider these inequalities unfair must be skeptical that their indefinite continuation is compatible with lasting peace—and wars, too, pollute.

There remains a need, however, to limit growth to those situations in which it contributes to human well-being. It is often the case that a pattern of "growth for growth's sake" occurs instead. The structure of some economic systems requires their participants to opt for continued economic growth, even when this growth does not improve living standards. The reasons for this include pressures of competition, individual risks of unemployment when growth slows down, and the desire by those whose privilege rests upon growth to sustain their position. This chapter explores the pressures for distorted and excessive growth that exist in capitalist economies and in centrally planned economic systems. A discussion of alternative economic institutions is also presented. The proposed institutions would create a more ecologically sound economy. The discussion will also assess the prospects facing efforts for ecological protection under present systems or for changes in the systems themselves.

AN INVITATION TO CONTROVERSY

The themes discussed in this chapter are controversial. The student who has read other books in this series will find disagreements here with some of their conclusions. In his book, *Prices and Markets*, Robert Dorfman expresses a fear that

> through lack of understanding of our delicate economic machine we should lose much that is valuable by incompetent attempts to correct much that is wrong. The main moral of this book must be that we have inherited a very delicate and subtle economic machine that has evolved slowly and painfully and without planning, and is still evolving. We can foster this evolution in desirable directions, or we can throw sand into the works. The better we understand the machine the less likely we are to damage it . . . If democratic institutions are precious, so is the economic system that seems to have fostered them.[1]

The author of this book is skeptical as to whether present economic institutions can solve our social and ecological problems, in part because they depend on incessant growth. Nor do I think that alternative democratic means of running an economy are necessarily impossible. The reader should not be surprised to find economists disagreeing. Despite common training, different individuals and generations bring to issues a variety of experiences and values. Any social scientist's observations naturally depend on the vantage point from which the object is viewed. The wisest course is to adopt the baseball umpire's motto, "I call 'em like I see 'em," and to count on readers to adopt it too. I believe the case for change is convincing.

Unnecessary Growth?

The very notion of unnecessary growth itself leads to controversy. Because different consumers vary in tastes, one may find something to be a wasteful

135

---

[1] Robert Dorfman, *Prices and Markets*, 2nd ed. (Englewood Cliffs ,N.J.: Prentice-Hall, Inc., 1972), pp. 257–58.

luxury that others consider necessary. Is art a luxury? Or golf? Or cigarettes? Or privacy? It requires some growth for any of these to be available widely. Is that growth necessary or not? There is no hard and fast rule. There may even be dispute over whether growth in the production of certain products is unnecessary, even if these products do not seem to contribute directly to consumer well-being.

Barry Commoner, for example, presents statistics showing that the production of many polluting products has increased faster than the growth of population, basic necessities, or even GNP itself. (See Table 7–1.) Increased pollution is not due to population growth or real consumer affluence, he argues, but to unnecessary growth, as polluting products replace natural and nonpolluting ones:

Table 7–1   CHANGES IN THE USE OF DIFFERENT PRODUCTS, 1946–1970, U.S.A.

Nonreturnable soda bottles	+53.000%
Synthetic fibers	+ 5,980%
Mercury (chlorine production)	+ 3,930%
Mercury (paint)	+ 3,120%
Air conditioner compressor units	+ 2,850%
Plastics	+ 1,960%
Fertilizer nitrogen	+ 1,050%
Electric housewares	+ 1,040%
Synthetic organic chemicals	+ 950%
Aluminum	+ 680%
Chlorine gas	+ 600%
Electric power	+ 530%
Pesticides	+ 390%
Wood pulp	+ 313%
Truck freight	+ 222%
Consumer electronics	+ 217%
Motor fuel consumption	+ 190%
Cement	+ 150%
Gross National Product	+ 126%
Population[a]	+ 42%
Railroad freight	+ 17%
Lumber	− 1%
Cotton fiber	− 7%
Returnable beer bottles	− 36%
Wool	− 42%
Soap	− 76%
Work animal horsepower	+ 87%

[a] Goods expanding at the pace of population, or between that rate and GNP Growth Rate not included. Among these are "food . . . total production of textiles and clothes, household utilities, and steel, copper and other basic metals."

Source: Barry Commoner, *The Closing Circle: Nature, Man and Technology* (New York: Alfred A. Knopf, 1971), p. 143.

The increase in population accounts for from 12 to 20 percent of the various increases in total pollutant output since 1946. The affluence factor (i.e., amount of economic good per capita) accounts for from 1 to 5 percent of the total increase in pollutant output, except in the case of passenger travel, where the contribution rises to about 40 percent . . . The technology factor—that is, the increased output of pollutants per unit production resulting from the introduction of new productive technologies since 1946—accounts for about 95 percent of the total output of pollutants, except in the case of passenger travel.[2]

Opponents might argue that Commoner underestimates increased affluence. If aluminum cans contribute to the drinker's happiness, is growing affluence measured by beer alone? Or must production of cans also be considered? (The case of passenger travel may cut the other way. The 40 percent figure measures increased automobile mileage, which may not represent rising commuter well-being, for reasons shown in Chapter 6.) Those who accept the affluence measurement may still claim the "technology factor" was necessary. Edwin L. Dale argues that population growth imposes a need to use more polluting methods because the increased number of consumers prevents supplies of old, nonpolluting materials from keeping up with demand.[3] This may sometimes be true, but an examination of some sectors such as transit shows instances in which it is not the case. Measuring exactly when growth is unnecessary may be difficult. Even if some cases are ambiguous, it appears that "growth for growth's sake" can sometimes occur. If it can, what is the effect of different economic systems on its probability?

PRESSURES FOR GROWTH UNDER CAPITALISM

A *capitalist economy* may be defined as a system in which most of the productive apparatus of society is owned by private, profit-seeking businesses. The production of different products, the division of labor, and the allocation of other resources are directed to some extent by the invisible hand of the market. In addition, the majority of the population earn a living from work for wages or salaries in businesses they do not themselves own.[4]

Pressures for growth under capitalism formed a major part of the analysis made by Karl Marx a century ago. He saw perpetual growth of wealth as the basic law of a system with separate classes of capitalists and wageworkers. To the capitalists he attributed strong desires to reinvest: "Accumulate. Accumulate. It is their Moses and their prophets."[5] Accumulation was not only the re-

[2] Barry Commoner, *The Closing Circle* (New York: Alfred A. Knopf, 1971), pp. 176–77.

[3] Edwin L. Dale, Jr., "The Economics of Pollution," *New York Times Magazine*, April 19, 1970.

[4] This definition excludes market economies in which most people work their own farms or small artisan businesses. Such an economy of the self-employed might suffer pollution from overuse of common waste-disposal resources, but it would not be forced to grow for the reasons discussed here.

[5] Karl Marx, *Capital* (1867) (New York: International Publishers, 1967), Vol. 1, p. 596.

sult of capitalist psychology. Each business was also forced to accumulate by competitive pressures. A business that did not grow and invest in advanced equipment would lose markets to its competitors. It would go bankrupt; its owners would lose their property and have to become wageworkers. The fear of this was sufficient to ensure that profits would be maximized and that most of them would be reinvested.

The drive for profits caused environmental problems in Marx's day. The effects of cutting costs at the expense of safety and environmental conditions were documented in accounts of British factory towns.[6] The accumulation of capital and the growth of cities, as farmers were driven from the land by enclosures, did more damage to water and air in factories and in nearby tenement districts than overgrazing could do to the commons of peasant villages. Nonetheless, Marx and Engels did not see growth as primarily negative in consequences. Capitalist accumulation, they always made clear, would build the productive capacity of society rapidly, allowing the eventual prosperity of the masses after capitalism had completed its historic mission of accumulation and been replaced.

In the twentieth century, capitalism has undergone some changes. Individual entrepreneurs have given way to large corporations with bureaucratic management structures. To some extent, competition between firms in product markets has been replaced by the semipeaceful coexistence of oligopolies. Government has new powers to control damages done by private interests. These changes reduce somewhat the necessity or ability of firms to cut costs continually by polluting others. Pressures for growth have not abated, however. The resulting rapid accumulation and technological change still can cause environmental damage. Several reasons for these pressures have been described.

Writers on ecological problems complain that people believe growth is automatically desirable. This faith, like the old "religious" drive for accumulation, is backed up by strong institutionalized incentives for growth. J. K. Galbraith has described some pressures that operate inside a corporate bureaucracy.[7] Each official is likely to be promoted if his own division grows in numbers of employees and amount of business handled. This is one source of pressure for expansion. In addition, the interests of shareholders and management employees must be compromised over the division of earnings. Shareholders will veto excessive salaries for the managers, and managers will limit the disbursement of dividends to owners. Reinvestment for growth is an obvious compromise. Even when managers are owners, funds are more likely to be reinvested than distributed. Personal incomes are subject to the income tax, although increases of wealth from the growth of the company are not immediately taxed (and are taxed at only half the rate if shares are later sold for a capital gain).

[6] Frederick Engels, *The Condition of the Working Class in England* (Oxford: Basil Blackwell, 1958). See also the novels of Charles Dickens.
[7] John Kenneth Galbraith, *The New Industrial State* (Boston: Houghton Mifflin, 1967).

The comparative growth rates of different firms are also important. A company that grows more slowly than others has trouble raising funds later if it does wish to expand. It also risks being taken over by more rapidly growing conglomerate firms, which can gain control by purchase of only some portion of the shares. Finally, if a company has expanded by borrowing rather than by reinvesting profits, it has an additional incentive to growth. Its fixed debts to banks may require an increase in sales if they are to be met. All these are factors that require growth of measured GNP, but they do not require that growth meet real needs of people. The new activities may be "unnecessary" growth.

These forces operate at the level of the individual firm. Economy-wide pressure for growth also operates through government action. Whenever capitalist economies are not growing rapidly, their governments feel a necessity to stimulate the economy. This has been particularly true since the Depression. Throughout the 1930s, private consumer and investment demand was insufficient to stimulate enough production for full employment or growth. Even a fall in wages and prices and the bankruptcy of competitors did not create enough opportunities to stimulate the surviving wealth holders to reinvest (as had occurred in earlier business cycles). Some economists argued that the consolidation of monopolies and the prior growth of government activities prevented the wave of bankruptcies from running its full course. Others, like Alvin Hansen, blamed slower population growth for weak demand. Some new source of demand had to be found, as J. M. Keynes pointed out. Governments could try to stimulate demand by their own public spending (or, in circumstances short of full-scale depression, by provision of easy money to private investors).[8]

The rapid end of the depression when government expenditure increased in World War II confirmed the diagnosis. Ever since, government has been seen as the guarantor of full employment. But how is government to expand employment? Government employment of large numbers of people on environmental or socially useful projects is possible. Some such projects were completed in the 1930s. Generally, these projects are not emphasized. Businesses demand their own activities be expanded faster to prevent the danger of bankruptcy. Large nonmilitary government projects are opposed by businesses that would face competition from specific projects. Even stimulation of private growth that would be more fitted to real social needs may be rejected because it would not increase profitability to the maximum in the short run. Companies prefer stimulation of the *most* growth, not the *best* growth. Government has usually found it expedient to follow this pressure. Most recessions are countered by special tax credits and other stimuli to private business expansion: growth of capacity, with its attendant increases in energy use and effluent production, generally is the result. Even the military budget, the largest source of direct government spending, is used to stimulate production in private companies.

139

[8] Alvin H. Hansen, *Full Recovery or Stagnation?* (New York: Norton, 1938); J. M. Keynes, *The General Theory of Employment, Interest and Money* (New York: Harcourt Brace, 1936).

International competition also requires governments to pursue a policy of stimulating growth. American businesses are forced to keep ahead of competitors in Japan and Europe; workers fear loss of jobs to foreign competition. The government must pursue policies of stimulating domestic investment instead of other employment—creating policies because of their effects on this international competition. It must listen to business arguments that tight antipollution standards would harm their international competitiveness.[9] Competition may lead countries to seek spheres of influence over different parts of the world from which they can exclude their rivals. Competition of different nations for investment opportunities, raw materials, and markets was a cause of the First World War. Protection of investment opportunities in less-developed countries from local rebellions and international rivals is sometimes cited as a cause of more recent wars. Wars, particularly with modern technology, are destructive of the environment.[10] The need to retain military strength in the face of competition is itself a reason why governments must pursue a policy of stimulating growth.

Programs for growth are usually politically popular. Individual workers, as well as businessmen, normally must support them because they need the incomes or jobs that growth creates. Demands on individuals for increased expenditure make the necessity greater. The incentives placed on each family to flee as far as possible to the suburbs, discussed in Chapter 6, create one case in which individuals must compete through higher spending. Tight labor markets often require that families give their children more education than others receive. The result is a competitive inflation of education costs. Communities must compete in job-producing industries with tax incentives and tax enforcement of pollution laws. Business desires to grow may also lead consumers to want more income. Manufacturers seeking growth are eager to advance consumer credit. Product changes, packaging, and advertising are used to convince consumers to buy more frequently.

Many economists are not convinced that these are significant factors in expanding demand. However, advertising is not the only means by which a capitalist system expands demand. The typical worker who does not own his own business is given little besides accumulation of consumer goods as a means of seeking satisfaction and displaying his worth. Craftsmanship and other forms of satisfaction from work are limited because the wageworker does not really control his own job. Competitive consumption is stimulated by the inequality of incomes that is also a feature of capitalism. The consumer's version of the rat race not only forces growth through expansion of demand; it also allows growth

[9] The United States would lose relatively less than its main rivals, Japan and Germany, if all countries tightened pollution controls. However, no one country dares to tighten standards if its competitors will not. See Ralph D'Arge, "Essay on Economic Growth and Environmental Quality" in P. Bohm and A. V. Kneese, *The Economics of Environment* (New York: St. Martin's, 1972).

[10] Barry Weisberg, ed., *Ecocide in Indochina* (San Francisco: Canfield Press, 1970); John Lewallen, *Ecology of Devastation: Indochina* (Baltimore: Penguin, 1971).

to continue by ensuring a continued supply of laborers to employers, even when the threat of starvation is no longer a factor.

For all of these reasons, workers, consumers, and local communities are often forced to advocate growth even when possibilities might exist for increasing well-being through programs requiring less business investment. It is another case, at times, of a prisoner's dilemma situation preventing collaboration on ecologically sound possibilities of ensuring full employment and adequate living standards. International or domestic competition may also make businesses advocate growth at times, although the resulting ecological damage and military expenditures may harm all business, taken together. At some times, businesses have combined to support government regulation that limited competition and allowed some environmental protection and conservation. Taken as a group, however, capitalist business may have more common interests in promoting growth than in limiting it for ecological reasons.

The principal element in modern capitalism, as it was in Marx's day, is the need for accumulation. Even if all of the greatest capitalist institutions, including the corporations and the banks, agreed among themselves and with the government on the need for environmental protection, they could not halt the growth of the economy without causing a fundamental change in their own basic mode of existence. Unless production is expanding, (or unless investment in labor-saving machinery is allowed to reduce the amount of wages paid) the magnitude of total profits cannot rise. If profit receivers wish to keep investing without a falling rate of return, zero growth is out.

Competition among individual businesses and among workers for jobs exerts automatic pressure for growth. If these pressures did not work, the capitalist institutions as a group would have to act in an open and political manner to stimulate growth or cease to be profit seeking in the way they have been since the beginnings of capitalism. Perhaps it is not surprising that although 57 percent of executives who answered a Fortune Magazine poll on ecology favored increased federal protection of the environment, 74 percent had stated that accelerated depreciation allowances, investment tax credits, or government grants for corporate abatement projects—all of which would increase growth—would be the "most effective" protection measures.[11]

PRESSURES FOR GROWTH WITH CENTRAL PLANNING

Problems of capitalism, including the difficulty of environmental control, have led to proposals for alternative economic systems. The "irrationality" of capitalist production, including external diseconomies and the extension of

---

[11] Cited in Richard England and Barry Bluestone, "Ecology and Class Conflict," *Review of Radical Political Economics*, Vol. 3, No. 4, Fall 1971, p. 48.

growth beyond people's needs, are traditional arguments for socialist central planning. Some environmental scientists also have suggested that power must be given to a scientific planner to save the world. However, even a central planning apparatus with considerable power will not necessarily improve the relationship of the economy and the environment. Problems arise both from the selection of goals by planners and from the incentives to induce compliance with plans. Central planning in Russia and Eastern Europe has not prevented environmental disruption. Water pollution is most serious. The Caspian Sea fish catch has fallen off. Several lakes and rivers are polluted by industrial plants. There have also been incidents of pipeline bursts and other forms of petroleum pollution. Air pollution is becoming a problem in some Eastern European cities, although greater dependence on public transport in the East than in the West has prevented this pollution from reaching crisis levels yet.[12]

One reason for this pollution is that the Soviet economies have been organized for the achievement of rapid growth at the cost of environmental protection. This may have been a deliberate choice, based on weighing the costs against the benefits of a possible higher future living standard and of the military defense that growth could ensure. Some critics within Eastern Europe, however, have argued that growth for the sake of growth has been built into their social system. They claim bureaucrats and planners in Eastern Europe have become a "new class," who, like the corporate managers and owners in capitalist countries, have a vested interest in growth.

The bureaucracy developed in a situation of economic crisis in which rapid growth was a social necessity. In Russia, this occurred after World War I and the 1917 revolution; in Eastern Europe, World War II had left the economies devastated. As two Polish critics state,

> Under such conditions, only industrialization can bring a real improvement of material, social and cultural conditions for the mass of the people in the cities and countryside . . . It was necessary to obtain maximum production and employment while maintaining consumption on a low level—production for production's sake.[13]

Thus, the planning bureaucracy developed its institutions around the goal of *production for production*. Internally, the incentives to individual bureaucrats to make their divisions grow were not too different from those described by Galbraith for the Western corporations. Externally, however, the planning system was only geared to forcing the economy to save. When industry had expanded, and factory workers, peasants, and technicians began to seek higher rates of consumption, there was no useful function left for the bureaucracy. To maintain its social position and power, the bureaucracy had to defend itself by enforcing

[12] Marshall I. Goldman, *The Spoils of Progress: Environmental Pollution in the Soviet Union* (Cambridge: MIT Press, 1972).

[13] Jacek Kuron and Karol Modzelewski, "An Open Letter to the Party," *New Politics*, Vol. 5, No. 2 and 3, 1968.

the goal of growth on the rest of society. The writers who have advanced this view have been concerned primarily with the lack of power and income permitted to the workers in this situation. Growth for the sake of growth also will have environmental effects similar to those of Western capitalism.

Even when growth is desired by the whole society, the organization of production by central planners also raises problems for avoiding excess pollution. The problem lies in the setting of goals for the many different factories and farms in society. If the planners use a monetary system or a bookkeeping analogue to a market and instruct enterprises to seek maximum profits, each unit will have an incentive to reduce its own costs even at the expense of others. Environmental external diseconomies will result. A similar result will occur if plant managers are simply given output quotas or told to produce as much as possible regardless of cost; the environment will be sacrificed in the many circumstances in which doing so will increase production of the specific product of the enterprise. Different goals or targets for factories—which would include reduction of environmental damage—are possible. They involve a more complex system of planning and monitoring firms. Even if such goals are nominally accepted, the individual plant managers or workers must know that these goals will affect chances of promotion or performances bonuses as much as total production before they can be effective.

These difficulties are not inevitable for a noncapitalist centrally planned system, in the way that externalities and a requirement of growth are for capitalism. Competition is not necessary to the system. A guarantee of employment for all can remove the incentive for workers to demand growth for the creation of jobs. Incentives for individual enterprises are not necessarily set in terms of profit, as they must be under a market economy. Incentives for conservation have been created in China, where the very scarcity of materials as well as concern for the environment has led to demands for recycling. However, there is no systematic pressure to ensure that ecologically damaging incentives, or simple planning errors, will not occur.

A planning system may also be subject to one additional problem. If the legitimacy of the planners, in the public's view, depends on their claim to expertise, the planners may have a strong incentive never to admit to mistakes. This would be particularly true in the case of a scientific ruling elite of the sort some ecologists have suggested. A system in which this happened might be unable either to correct some planning errors or to alter its course from growth to stability, if it had first pursued growth.

The orientation of a planning bureaucracy to production for production may depend on who the planners are and on the basis of their claim to legitimacy. If the whole populace were to do the planning democratically, rather than leaving the job to a planning bureaucracy, the problem might not arise. To raise this possibility, however, is to discuss economies that go beyond current economic systems. The possibilities for new institutional systems involving democratic planning or decentralized decisions without external damage or pressure for

143

accumulation are still in the realm of utopian thought. These speculations, however, are important enough for human welfare and ecological survival that they may be reported.

NONHIERARCHICAL ALTERNATIVES

Visions of an ecologically sound, humane economy have been advanced by people who call themselves socialists, anarchists, and even conservatives. Despite the variety of the visionaries, their programs have some common elements. Hierarchical systems of ownership and control are rejected, whether they involve power by owners of capital over workers, or power by noncapitalist planners over workers. In addition, extreme specialization in the division of labor and separation between urban areas and rural hinterlands are rejected in these visions of alternative systems.

Some reasons advanced for opposing hierarchy are based on desires for equality or freedom, and will not be elaborated here. There are, however, direct ecological arguments that have been raised against hierarchical economic systems. Colonial control creates ecological problems of the sort seen in the discussion of Java. As the discussions of capitalism and centralized planning showed, competition for places in the hierarchy and a need to legitimize their positions or to buy off opposition may force elites to pursue rapid growth.

In addition, the division of production, so that some give orders and others follow them on the job, requires an often rigid division of labor. Job descriptions become simplified and factories and agricultural regions are led to specialize in particular products, either by competition that requires costs be cut to a minimum or because managers wish to simplify their own tasks of supervision. The specialization of agricultural regions in single crops, by simplifying ecosystems, creates dangers of plant epidemics and other ecological problems discussed in Chapter 3. Large and specialized factories can increase concentrations of specific pollutants in small areas to dangerous levels. Regional specialization also increases the costs of transporting goods from one place to another. The growth of large bureaucracies to control production itself is an ecological hazard because the centers of control tend to become large cities with their own pollution problems.[14]

A lack of control over working conditions and society by those at the bottom of the hierarchy also can lead to feelings of dissatisfaction. So can the division of labor itself, by depriving work of any sense of craftsmanship or control over products. Capitalist competition or the decisions of planners may cause changes in the division of labor and destroy permanent communities that could be another source of satisfaction. Competition may also lead people to see others

[14] Stephen Hymer, "The Multinational Corporation and the Law of Uneven Development," in *Economics and World Order*, J. N. Bhagwati, ed. (New York: Macmillan, 1972).

as opponents, rather than friends. The dissatisfaction or "alienation" fostered by these pressures often leaves people with no sources of satisfaction apart from those available from consumer goods. Thus, more production and growth may seem necessary than would be the case if people had stable communities and real control and participation in the decisions of production.[15]

As against this hierarchical division of labor, anarchists have often spoken of self-governing balanced regional economies. Presumably these would be relatively self-sufficient economies, containing both industrial and agricultural activities. Some trade might occur between these regions, but most of their needs would be met by their own work. Similarly, Marx and Engels wrote of the need to abolish the "antithesis between town and country" as part of the abolition of the exploitation of labor by capital.[16] Marx argued that ancient cities had lived off the surplus produced by a subservient countryside, and the first capitalists, developing in the cities, had secured a wage labor force by separating peasants from the land. Most Marxists have held that the growth of towns was itself desirable because it ended the isolation of peasant life, and have envisioned a somewhat more industrial version of the utopian society than have the anarchists. However, the Marxist governments of Cuba and China have expressed aspirations for the decentralization of population and industry into rural areas.

Religious and nationalist movements have sometimes also held similar ideals. Ghandi wished to preserve or restore peasant village society in India as the basis of a nonhierarchical society. The *kibbutz* in Israel merges religious tradition with a self-governing socialist organization of independent rural communities that mix farming with industrial activities. Even conservatives have often been attracted by the vision of a country of yeoman farmers, and, for the believer in competitive market economies, the large organization of any sort has sometimes been an enemy. Some free-market economists argue that only government protection allows monopolies to exist and argue for anarchism, rather than antitrust laws, as a defense against hierarchy. Socialists would argue that capitalist firms themselves would frustrate this by recreating the government, but some conservatives nonetheless harken back to Jefferson's warnings against the growth of cities and extend them into a vision much like that of anarchism or decentralized socialism.

Technology without Hierarchy?

If hierarchy and extreme specialization are abandoned, some people feel technology and increasing living standards will also have to be abandoned. Although some utopian thinkers reject modern technology entirely or are willing to sacrifice modern production to achieve other social goals, few people would follow them in a search that would require not only zero, but negative, GNP

[15] Ellen Willis, "Consumerism and Women," *Socialist Revolution*, Vol. 1, No. 3, May 1970, pp. 76–82.

[16] Frederick Engels, *The Housing Question* (1872) (New York: International Publishers, n.d.).

growth. Some proponents of a nonhierarchical economy, however, claim that hierarchy could be ended without reducing living standards. Modern methods of communication and production could be adapted to other economic systems.

Much of existing equipment was developed for use in large factories, large farms, and large bureaucracies. Indeed, the factory came before the industrial revolution. The first factories were not devised to increase productivity through large scale operations or a division of labor. Rather, they allowed capitalists to supervise workers more closely, to prevent loafing or pilferage. At first, each weaver in a factory tended his own loom, as earlier weavers had done in their cottages. Only later was more productive mechanized equipment developed for the factory. With this increase in productivity, an industrial revolution was started.[17]

However, science can be applied in new directions. Over time, advanced technology has developed to the point at which it is sometimes predicted that the factory will disappear. Marshall MacLuhan predicts more versatile machine tools that could create a variety of consumer goods.[18] Development of agriculture in Japan and the Netherlands, where land is scarce, suggests possibilities of highly developed technology for small farms producing a variety of crops. They might also be made less hierarchical:

> the new technology, because it exercises interaction, implies greater *interdependence* but not necessarily a hierarchical structure. Communication linkages could be arranged in the form of a grid in which each point was directly connected to many other points permitting lateral communication as well as vertical communication . . . Such a grid is made more feasible by aeronautical and electronic revolutions which greatly reduce costs of communications. It is not technology which creates inequality, rather it is organization that imposes a ritual judicial asymmetry on the use of intrinsically symmetrical means of communications and arbitrarily creates unequal capacities to initiate and terminate exchange, to store and retrieve information, and to determine the extent of the exchange and the terms of the discussion.[19]

The assembly line, the giant agribusiness planting large tracts to individual crops, the bureaucracy processing large amounts of information on computers for purposes of control represents one use of modern technology, but not the only possible use.

Murray Bookchin has described one technological alternative for use in an anarchist regional economy. He argues such economies would allow food cultivation to be adapted to the conditions of the region, rather than to the scheduling imperatives of corporate organization. Similarly, they would allow for new energy sources, as well as economizing on energy use for transportation or un-

[17] S. M. Marglin, "What Do Bosses Do?," working paper of the Harvard University Department of Economics, 1971.

[18] Marshall MacLuhan, *Understanding Media: The Extensions of Man* (New York: McGraw-Hill, 1964), Chap. 33.

[19] Hymer, *op. cit.*

necessary production. "The Industrial Revolution increased the quantity of energy available to industry, but it diminished the variety of energy resources used by man," he states. Modern techniques for harnessing wind, solar power, or tides are available but do not concentrate much energy in one place. They cannot supply large cities with energy except at a prohibitive cost in energy transmission. In smaller regional economies, Bookchin believes, they can be used. In addition, he argues smaller cities would allow a substitution of short-range electric vehicles for gasoline powered cars in urban transportation. A more dispersed population could even burn some fossil fuels without local concentration of pollutants becoming a problem.[20]

Coordination, Allocation, and Incentives

Even a nonhierarchical economy would require some trade between its regions, if it were to use sophisticated technology. Even if rural-urban differences were reduced, and each region produced its basic necessities, some degree of specialization would be required. This trade and specialization would require coordination among the regions. In addition, if the economy envisioned was faced with a scarcity of resources and if the limited amount of labor that people would voluntarily contribute for the pleasure of working did not provide for the material wants of the community, methods of allocating goods and incentives to effort would be required. The needs for coordination, allocation, and incentive mechanisms might not be as great as in present-day economies, particularly if participation in decisions over production and the social organization of communities made work less onerous and provided alternative means of satisfaction besides consumer goods. Nonetheless, some institutions for motivating work, distributing products, and coordinating effort would be required.

Economic theory knows of two basic methods to achieve these ends: planning and markets. In the abstract, either method can be thought of as compatible with a nonhierarchical society. Each, however, also poses dangers.

A market, or price system, can direct goods from one place to another and give signals as to whether more or less production is warranted. Prices can ration scarce resources, and market payments can give material incentives for effort by individuals or communities. Conservative critics and Yugoslav-style market socialists alike can think of a price system linking small towns or communes, each of which has internal institutions allowing social solidarity, and each of which is subjected to rules requiring them to consider as costs any damage to the environment. Conservatives and anarchists also favor the market as a means for avoiding the hierarchical handing of orders from planners to followers. A market, however, has some built-in tendencies to create hierarchies. A few lucky or ambitious communities or individuals may get ahead of the others; before long they are reinventing government interference with the market to protect

147

[20]Murray Bookchin, *Post-Scarcity Anarchism* (Berkely: Ramparts Press, 1971), pp. 55–140.

their privileges. A market system without inequality is not a self-regulating mechanism that can work automatically forever.

Planning can also allocate resources and coordinate production. However, it involves some dangers of the rise of a caste of planners. A number of systems for democratic control over planning have been proposed, involving election and rotation in office and government by a confederation of regional or local democracies, with power at the top limited to issues that cannot be solved locally. Democratic institutions for the selection of planners cannot long ensure, however, that, once selected, planners will not consolidate their position somehow. Planners also need to induce people to follow their plans. Force, material incentives, and persuasion seem to be the only three possibilities. Institutions for democratic planning clearly require that there be no organs of force given to the planners. To forbid the use of wages for controlling the population, however, may prevent use of desirable incentives for effort on needed, but unpopular, tasks. A system of planning and selecting planners is not a self-regulating mechanism that can work automatically forever, either.

This lack of one automatic mechanism to run the economy is not, however, a fatal flaw. The vision of an ecologically sound, humane economy need not demand an alternative invisible hand to that of capitalism. If people can exercise choice—and Chapter 1 showed this is a basic assumption that differentiates economics from other sciences—they need not choose a system that will run itself. One can think of a system that would work as long as people are agreed to act deliberately when tendencies toward reestablishment of a hierarchy of wealth or planning appear.

Such a system might mix some elements of market coordination with elements of planning. It might, in practice, bear some similarity to present experiments with communal production for outside markets, as practiced in the *kibbutz* or *moshav* in Israel. It might use the market to coordinate community owned or worker controlled enterprises, a system with which Yugoslavia has made some experiments. It might adopt some of the basic institutions of planning now used in other socialist countries, but substitute democratic control over planning for control by political party bureaucracies. It might not resemble any present-day experiments at all. The details of possible systems will probably not be derived by theoretical speculation. Attempts to create such a system will show, in their successes and failures, exactly what will or will not work. All we can predict is that such a system, as it utilizes elements of either markets or planning, will require people to be aware of the dangers of hierarchy as well as of the needs of the economy. Under the best of institutions, it will still be true that "eternal vigilance is the price of liberty." Such vigilance, however, will be easier in an economy in which hierarchy is absent than in one in which it already exists.

Eternal vigilance, too, may be the price of ecological soundness in the nonhierarchical economy. Market elements used in the system will create some incentives to overuse common resources. Planners will make mistakes, some of which might involve environmental disruption. Nonetheless, this vigilance, too, will be easier in a decentralized and nonhierarchical economy than it is under present-day capitalism or bureaucratic central planning. If a nonhierarchical economy can be organized and standards of living are sufficiently high, a number of the ecological problems of contemporary economic systems will be absent. Previous chapters showed several ways in which the prevalence of inequality makes environmental protection difficult. It may deter the spread of information on methods of limiting conception and thus make population pressures worse. It can lead to the ecological simplification of agriculture and the large-scale use of pesticides instead of more labor intensive systems of biological control because of the need to simplify routine on large farms. It can lead to a flight of the poor from the land and a drawing of huge populations to the cities from which corporate or bureaucratic control is exercised. It can add to the flight to the suburbs by the wealthy within those cities, increasing burdens to the environment from commuting. It can lead to competitive consumption, competitive armament, and unlimited drives to accumulate, motivated by fear of falling behind within a system of inequality or by a lack of alternative satisfactions besides consumer goods.

These ecological drawbacks of a hierarchical economy outweigh whatever virtues Malthus found in "misery." A nonhierarchical system would not guarantee perfect environmental protection, but it would at least remove these specific pressures. An "ecological consciousness" on the part of the population might still be required to preserve the environment, but it would face fewer obstacles than such a concern for nature faces under current institutional systems.

THE STRUGGLE FOR ENVIRONMENTAL PROTECTION

A utopian economy that would pose fewer threats to the environment than capitalism or bureaucratic planning is an interesting exercise for the economist's imagination. When contrasted to present economies, it helps clarify ways in which the latter threaten ecological balance. The vision may also inspire efforts to improve the economy and the environment. However, there is also a danger in utopian thought.

The contrast between a utopian system and present-day economies may be so great as to create a feeling that any improvement is impossible unless change is total. On the other hand, lack of detail in the utopian vision, and the recognition that even a nonhierarchical economy would require a vigilant public to confront its problems, makes it hard to convince people to change society totally. Even if discontents with the present society are great, a prisoner's dilemma situation inhibits broader changes.

Barrington Moore, a historian of revolutions, has tried to explain why **149** people often accept a "society nobody wants." Even revolutions that everyone desires, except perhaps a few rulers, are rare, because of the risks in starting them. Moore argues only part of the obstacle to change is the "superior force, authority and prestige" of kings, owners of capital, bureaucratic planners or other rulers:

> There were enough of us to smash *that* any time we wanted to, and there are right now. The moment we stopped being good citizens [and] used our heads a trifle, the whole idiotic show would come to a stop . . . Such fantasies are no doubt common enough. But every 'sensible' person knows they are fantasies, that he is too busy making a living, that the risk is too great . . . Because of the stake he has in his society there is always substantial short-term rationality in being the good citizen. That short-term rationality leads to larger results that are totally absurd is obvious enough to require no elaboration.[21]

Because each person finds the costs of seeking change great, and the vision of a possible better society so unclear, nobody makes the effort, even though if everyone did, a better society would be assured. So we may get a "society that nobody wants"—and an environment that satisfies nobody.

Change is also difficult because real short-term conflicts of interest divide those with a stake in long-term change. In the area of ecology, this is particularly clear. Consumers oppose banning DDT because they fear food prices will rise; refinery workers oppose conservation programs to defend their jobs; low income automobile commuters oppose effluent charges on gasoline; taxpayers would lose if government spending for environmental improvements rose; incomes may rise in the short run from growth due to environmentally destructive military projects; and so on. No environmental reform appears to have a chance, given these divisions. As a result, the effort to organize movements for reform is sometimes not made.

Action, however, is not always futile. Several different reforms might be combined with guaranteed full employment; work on environmental projects might be financed by closing tax loopholes now used to stimulate corporate growth for growth's sake. Such a program would face corporate opposition, but a strong movement of all possible beneficiaries might make it politically feasible.

In recent years, a movement to defend the environment has begun in the United States and in other countries. This movement has not, however, proposed many such coalitions. Often, it has stressed individual levels of action, adopting the idea that personal misbehavior—having too many children, abandoning beer cans, consuming too much, or otherwise overusing common resources—is to blame. The comment of the cartoon character, Pogo, "We have met the enemy, and they are us," is often quoted.[22]

This view neglects completely the role of the economic system in shaping the incentives and options that face individuals. It may also engender a sense of guilt that inhibits action. When ecological movements have stressed political change rather than individual abstention, they have often been too narrow in

150

[21] Barrington Moore, Jr., "The Society Nobody Wants," in K. H. Wolff and B. Moore, *The Critical Spirit* (Boston: Beacon Press, 1967), pp. 410–11.
[22] Walt Kelley, *Impollutable Pogo* (New York: Simon and Schuster, 1970).

their scope to overcome short-run differences of interest. This does not, however, mean that a successful ecological movement is impossible.

If fear of unemployment, higher prices, or increased taxes keeps people from supporting them, broader coalitions, with wider sets of demands, may still allow for successful reform efforts. If there is opposition by direct beneficiaries of pollution, a major organizing effort may confront them successfully. Any effort at organization does involve risk. However, seeking such organization may be worth the risk. Game theorists' studies of the prisoner's dilemma indicate that even though risks keep people from the best possible outcome in some cases, if a "game" is repeated often enough the "players" may eventually see their common interest. Enough begin to take risks to signal to others that change in the outcome is possible.

An effective ecological reform movement might begin through the organization of people with long-run common interests in change, and the overcoming of short-run differences and risks. Such a movement would face continuing difficulties due to the pressures for environmentally unsound growth that exist under capitalism and to prisoner's dilemma situations that divide potential beneficiaries. It would also face the opposition of owners of capital who benefit most from current arrangements, just as a movement in a bureaucratically planned economy would face the opposition of the bureaucratic planning establishment. The movement, as it grew, might eventually find it easier to institute a completely new economic system than to continue fighting old institutions. If, in the process, it came to advocate a nonhierarchical ordering of the economy, it might find allies whose primary concern would be equality or an absence of control of decisions from above. The end result might be the kind of society that now seems a utopian dream, far too vague to inspire the risks of organization.

The emergence of a vision of a new society from concrete efforts for short-term reform may be the only possible route to social change. It seems more likely to work than positing an overall utopian blueprint. Some initial bases in building coalitions and inspiring effort must, however, be found. As environment problems come to harm more people, ecological issues may become possible bases for such coalitions.

A call for reform efforts that recognizes that coalitions for immediate reform may grow into movements for new economic systems is the conclusion that emerges from this analysis. However, the full analysis need not be accepted to arrive at a recommendation of action. Even if pollution, resource depletion, or inadequate food supply are not the result of the overall structure of the economic system, organization will be required to overcome them. If all that is needed is to remove imperfections in a basically sound system of property rights, an ecological movement should lead easily to effluent charges, regulation of common resources, or whatever other fine tuning is necessary. More complex reforms of urban settlement and transportation, agricultural production, or recycling technology could also be stimulated by the pressure of such a movement, where they would be unlikely in its absence.

151

If, however, reform efforts are constantly confronted by continuing pressures for unnecessary growth and continued divisions of interest among potential beneficiaries, broader coalitions and broader visions of change will have to be developed. In this sense, a movement for change is a kind of scientific experiment. It tests out exactly how much must be done for its goals to be achieved. It demonstrates in practice what pressures are generated in an economic system. Economic theory alone can never give a definitive answer as to whether the present economic mechanism can solve environmental problems or whether this system can and should be replaced. Only time and experience will prove whether such a change is necessary or possible.

The social scientist, however, must be permitted to predict a most likely outcome. The author shares *neither* the view that present market institutions of capitalism, if left undisturbed, will operate effectively, *nor* the technocratic faith that a perfect central planner can be found. Still less, do I accept Malthus' view that misery is inevitable and that reform only makes it worse. I believe that the overwhelming majority of humanity can do better, for themselves and for the balance between economies and ecosystems, than their past rulers have done for them.

SUMMARY

It is unusual for an economics textbook to conclude that struggles for social change are needed. This does not mean it is unusual for texts to have an implicit political moral. A statement that current institutions are worth preserving is also political. Nonetheless, the environmental crisis suggests that current economic institutions are not compatible with either the interests of most people or the continued balance between man's activities and natural ecosystems. Both capitalist economies and bureaucratic planning systems enforce patterns of growth for growth's sake on the economy, as well as organizing society in a hierarchical form that may be undesirable for other reasons. The dependence of these systems on growth, combined with other institutional imperfections discussed in previous chapters, endangers the environment. A nonhierarchical organization of the economy, involving some elements of planning and of a price system with popular concern for equality, liberty, and the environment might reduce some of these threats to nature, although it would still require a population vigilant to protect both liberty and the environment. Such an organization seems utopian at present. It might be attained as the end result of a movement for change that began with attempts to build coalitions for specific ecological reforms, but which admitted the possibility that overall reorganization of the economy might be necessary. I believe such a movement is worth attempting.

In the comparative structure of different economies, see Gregory Grossman, *Comparative Economic Systems*, in this series, and Howard Sherman, *Radical Political Economics* (New York: Basic Books, 1972). Further critique of the capitalist economy is found in Richard Edwards, Michael Reich, and Thomas Weisskopf, *The Capitalist System* (Englewood Cliffs, N.J.: Prentice-Hall, Inc., 1972); the historical critiques of how the Soviet economy became dependent on growth include Leon Trotsky, *The Revolution Betrayed* (New York: Merit, 1965); Milovan Djilas, *The New Class* (New York: Praeger, 1956); and Raya Dunayevskaya, *Marxism and Freedom* (New York: Bookman Associates, 1958). Some critical analyses of capitalism, particularly Paul Baran and Paul Sweezy, *Monopoly Capital* (New York Monthly Review Press, 1966), argue the system has a tendency toward stagnation, a claim that may appear to contradict the argument that it is dependent on growth. The stagnation referred to may, however, be in employment and useful production, not in resource use and total put-through, so the two critiques are not necessarily contradictory.

Critiques of ecological policy under capitalism include James Ridgeway, *The Politics of Ecology* (New York: Dutton, 1971); Barry Weisberg, *Beyond Repair, The Ecology of Capitalism* (Boston: Beacon Press, 1971); Editors of Ramparts, *Eco-Catastrophe* (San Francisco: Canfield Press, 1970); and, covering earlier periods, Samuel P. Hays, *Conservation and the Gospel of Efficiency* (Cambridge: Harvard University Press, 1959). The role of values in social science is treated in Gunnar Myrdal, *Objectivity in Social Research* (New York: Pantheon, 1969). For the vision of a nonhierarchical economy, see Percival and Paul Goodman, *Communitas* (New York: Vintage Books, 1960), and Murray Bookchin, *Post-Scarcity Anarchism* (Berkeley: Ramparts Press, 1971).

157

Forests:
    agriculture in, 31, 33
    commercial, 24
    fur trade and, 7
"Forests: The Habit of Waste" (Malcolm
    Margolin), 24n
Forms of pollution (*table*), 64, 65n
Forrester, Jay W., 66, 66n, 68
"Free Transit" (Gerald Kraft and Thomas
    Domencich), 115n
Full Recovery or Stagnation (Alvin H.
    Mansen), 139n
"Fun and Games with Gross National
    Product: The Role of Misleading
    Indicators in Social Policy" (Kenneth
    E. Boulding), 73n

G

Galbraith, J. K., 129n, 138, 138n
Geertz, Clifford, 52n
Generalized species, 18
*General Theory of Employment, Interest,
    and Money, The* (J. M. Keynes),
    139n
Ghandi, 145
Goldman, Marshall, I., 142n
Great Transformation, The (Karl Polanyi),
    62n
Green Revolution, 45–48
"Green Revolution: Cornucopia or Pandora's
    Box?" (Clifton R. Wharton), 47n
Gross National Product (GNP):
    measurement problems, 69–74
    zero growth argument, 66–69
Growth:
    arithmetic and doubling rates, 27, 67
    capitalist, 137–41
    with central planning, 141–44
    economic, uses of, 43–45
    economic limits to, 66–69
    of food production, 43–48, 52–54
    for growth's sake, 134
    of population, 27–40
    of specific products, 136
    structural change and, 17–21
    of systems, 17–20
    urban, effects on pollution, 61

H

Haeckel, Ernst, 6
Hagen, E. E., 63n
Hansen, Alvin, 139, 139n
Hardesty, John, 68n

Hardin, Garrett, 50n, 51
"Harvest of the Seas" (George
    Borgstrom), 49n
Hawrylyshyn, O., 63n
"Health and Air Pollution" (Lester B. Lave
    and Eugene P. Seskin), 104n
Heat:
    from pipelines, 127
    as pollution, 64–65
Henning, J. A., 104n
Hierarchy:
    alternatives to, 144–49
    capitalist, 137–41
    planning, 141–44
    urban congestion and, 117n
Hot Oil Act, 127
Housing Question, The (Frederick Engels),
    145n
Hunt, E. K., 107n
Hydrocarbon pollutants, 64–65, 113, 116
Hymer, Stephen, 59n, 144n

I

Impollutable Pogo (Walt Kelley), 150n
Incentives:
    agricultural institutions and, 51–52
    in bureaucracies, 142
    commons and, 48–51
    farmer response, 46
    to limit pollution, 93–103
    market, 2–4, 14
    to spread information, 39
Inequality:
    of antipollution incentives, 97–98, 101–3
    effect on populations, 31, 40
"Innovative Supply: A Weak Point in
    Economic Development Theory"
    (Matthew Edel), 16n
Input-output:
    defined, 11–13
    flows in an economy (*table*), 12
    material balances and, 69, 72
    United States, 69–71
    value calculation, 13
Institutions, economic:
    capitalist, 137–41
    central planning, 141–44
    evolution of, 20
    food supply and, 46–48
    to limit externality, 92–102
    nonhierarchical, 144–49
    petroleum industry, 124–28
    population and, 32
    social cost and, 80–83
"International Ladies Garment Workers
    Union," 81n
Irish potato famine, 32

159

P

Panel of Technical Advisers on Automotive Air Pollution, 114n
"Pangloss on Pollution" (E. J. Mishan), 106n
Parasites, 45
Pecuniary externalities, definition, 76
Peril on the Job (Ray Davidson), 81
Pesticides, effects of, 46
Petroleum:
 input in consumer goods and services (*table*), 71
 input in goods demanded by final user sectors (*table*), 70
Petroleum industry, 125–31
Pigs for the Ancestors (Roy A. Rappaport), 33n
Planning:
 central, 141–44
 and markets, 147–49, 152
Plant epidemics, 46
Plants, diseases of, 29–30, 45
Polanyi, Karl, 62, 62n, 79, 80
"Political Economy of Environmental Destruction, The" (John Hardesty, Norris C. Clement, and Clinton E. Jencks), 68n
Pollution (*see also* Air pollution, Water pollution, and Food chains):
 benefits, definition, 86
 cost and benefit, measurement of, 88–89
 costs, definition, 86
 definition of optimal level, 88
 forms (*table*), 64–65
 link to GNP, 69
 regulation, historical, 61–62, 107–8, 126–27
 by visible objects, 64–65, 107–8
 water levels, 89
"Poor Laws," 4–5
"Population Question in Northeastern Brazil, The" (Herman E. Daly), 39n
"Population" (Richard A. Easterlin), 35n
Populations, animal:
 cattle (*fig.*), 2–3
 goats, Townshend's, 4–5
 lynx, 2–3
 regulation of, 16–17
 salmon, 21–22
 snowshoe hare (*fig.*), 2
Populations, human:
 birthrate decline, 55
 deliberate regulation, 37–40
 effects on, 2–3, 5, 34–35
 graphical analysis, 28–29, 37, 43–45
 Japan, 54–55
 Java, 52–54

Populations, human (*cont.*)
 maximum potential size, 41–42
 regulation:
  by hunger, 28–31
  by misery, 27–28, 66
  by plague, 29–30
  resource balance (*fig.*), 29
  theories of regulation, 5, 27–28
Positive checks, 31–32
Postan, Michael, 29, 29n, 39
Preventive checks, 31–32
Prices:
 determination by supply and demand, 14–16
 ecological effects on, 7–8, 29–30
 petroleum, 126–27
 signal to producers, 3–4
 urban transport, 113–24
Prices and Markets (Robert Dorfman), 135n
Primary consumers, 10
Prisoner's dilemma:
 defined, 117
 countervailing power and, 129
 possibility of overcoming, 151
 sustaining capitalism, 141, 149–52
 transportation and, 117
Property rights (*see also* Common resources):
 and externality, 77
 and pollution, 92–103
Public goods:
 definition, 109
 environment as, 108–9
"Pure Theory of Public Expenditure, The" (Paul A. Samuelson), 109n

R

Radioactivity:
 nuclear testing, 105, 108
 as pollution, 64–65
"Raping Alaska: The Ecology of Oil" (Barry Weisberg), 129n
Rappaport, Roy, 33, 33n
Recycling:
 alternative to pollution, 72
 natural, 60
Reform, strategy for, 149–52
Regulating of pollution, 93–96
Report to the Joint State Government Commission (Panel of Technical Advisers on Automotive Air Pollution), 114n
Ricardo, David, 27, 32–33, 55
Ridker, R. G., 104n
Rockfeller, John D., 125
Ryan, William, 118n

161

W

Wages, effects of population growth, 29–30, 39
Walters, A. A., 119n
Water pollution:
  costs and benefits, 89–92
  Delaware River, 89–92
  East Europe, 142
  forms of, 64–65
  measurement, 89–92

Water pollution *(cont.)*
  oil spills, 127, 130
  Ruhr Valley, 108
  strategies for control, 89
Wealth of Nations, The (Adam Smith), 5
Weisberg, Barry, 129n, 140n
Wharton, Clifton R., Jr., 47n
Williamson, H. F., 115n
Willis, Ellen, 145n
Wohl, M., 124n
Working conditions, 80–82
  pollution of, 81–82
World Dynamics (J. W. Forrester), 66n